STUDIES ON INDUSTRIAL PRODUCTIVITY: SELECTED WORKS

Volume 5

FLEXIBLE MANUFACTURING SYSTEMS

FLEXIBLE MANUFACTURING SYSTEMS
Planning Issues and Solutions

ZUBAIR M. MOHAMED

Routledge
Taylor & Francis Group

LONDON AND NEW YORK

First published in 1994 by Garland Publishing Inc.

This edition first published in 2019
by Routledge
2 Park Square, Milton Park, Abingdon, Oxon OX14 4RN

and by Routledge
711 Third Avenue, New York, NY 10017

Routledge is an imprint of the Taylor & Francis Group, an informa business

British Library Cataloguing in Publication Data
A catalogue record for this book is available from the British Library

ISBN: 978-1-138-61548-9 (Set)
ISBN: 978-0-429-44077-9 (Set) (ebk)
ISBN: 978-1-138-31473-3 (Volume 5) (hbk)
ISBN: 978-0-429-45671-8 (Volume 5) (ebk)

Publisher's Note
The publisher has gone to great lengths to ensure the quality of this reprint but
points out that some imperfections in the original copies may be apparent.

Disclaimer
The publisher has made every effort to trace copyright holders and would welcome
correspondence from those they have been unable to trace.

FLEXIBLE MANUFACTURING SYSTEMS

Planning Issues and Solutions

ZUBAIR M. MOHAMED

GARLAND PUBLISHING, Inc.
New York & London / 1994

Library of Congress Cataloging-in-Publication Data

Mohamed, Zubair M., 1957–
    Flexible manufacturing systems : planning issues and solutions /
Zubair M. Mohamed.
        p.   cm. — (Garland studies on industrial productivity)
    Includes bibliographical references and index.
    ISBN 0–8153–1630–5
    1. Flexible manufacturing systems—Planning.   2. Production
planning.   I. Title. II. Series.
TS155.6.M64   1994
670.42'7—dc20   94–484
                                                                   CIP

Printed on acid-free, 250-year-life paper
Manufactured in the United States of America

Dedicated to:

my parents

                Rasheed and Zahara

my family

                Nishath, Farhan, and Abrar

Contents

Preface

The rapidly changing customer needs and intense competition are driving today's industry to introduce new products and improve the existing ones more frequently than ever. This trend has led to shorter product life cycles, frequent design changes, and smaller work-in-process and finished goods inventories. Consequently, over 90% of today's production is manufactured in lots of less than 50 parts, which renders application of dedicated production lines uneconomical. To remain competitive, the industry is adapting flexible manufacturing systems (FMSs) to produce these low- to medium-volume batch sizes. The objective is the timely production of parts with superior quality at low cost. However, it has been found that FMSs in the United States are under-utilized in terms of flexibility and capacity. In this book among other issues, production planning decisions are analyzed with respect to their impact on capacity utilization and system flexibility.

A flexible manufacturing system is a state of the art production system in which the movement of parts, tool loading/unloading, and processing of parts are controlled by a computer. In addition, the computer continuously updates the status on job progress, monitors tool wear/break and machine break-down, and signals a corrective action when needed.

Robots and numerical control machines contained in an FMS are designed to be flexible, self-contained, and can perform in a "stand-alone" environment. Integration of this hardware to form an FMS has brought forth various problems. These problems can be classified into two categories: design problems and operational problems. Design problems are concerned with the selection of parts to be made in FMS, selection of types of machines and their numbers, selection of material handling systems, facility layout, and other long-term factors. Operational problems are short-term (e.g., day-to-day) and are concerned with the operation of an FMS, which include production planning and scheduling.

This book takes a holistic approach to production planning problems. Specifically, it undertakes a comprehensive study dealing with the effects of machine flexibility, tool magazine capacity, varying production demands, and different operating policies on the production planning problems: part grouping, part routing, and machine loading. Performance measures such as FMS flexibility, makespan, and inventory are used in evaluating the effects. Three measures of FMS flexibility: actual routing flexibility, potential routing flexibility, and capacity flexibility are defined and operationalized.

Two operating policies are used in the development of loading and routing models. One model incorporates the needs of the FMS users: due-date satisfaction, low inventory holdings, and efficient system utilization, and the other reflects the popular maximize production rate objective widely prevalent in the research literature. The policy developed to reflect the needs of the FMS users is termed minimum cost policy. Simulation studies involving 320 replications of short run production requirements for 32 FMS environments provide important insights into the operation of an FMS. The results show that the minimum cost policy results in significantly lower inventory with higher routing flexibility without statistically affecting the systems capacity, flexibility, or the planned makespan. However, the maximum production rate policy was found to be more sensitive to tool magazine capacity and to variations in production requirements than the minimum cost policy.

The author takes full responsibility for the research findings and conclusions reported in this book.

Zubair M. Mohamed
Bowling Green, Kentucky

Acknowledgments

I thank my family, Nishath, Farhan, and Abrar for putting up with me during the long periods of solitude. I would also like to acknowledge the support and spirit my parents, Zahara and Rasheed, inculcated in me to travel overseas in the pursuit of knowledge. I thank John J. Bernardo of University of Kentucky for his invaluable support and guidance that he provided from the inception to the completion of this book.

I

Flexible Manufacturing Systems

1.1 INTRODUCTION

International and domestic competition coupled with changing customer needs and shorter product life cycles are requiring U.S. manufacturers to overhaul their operations. Firms must react to market changes quickly with better quality products at low cost. To cope with this new environment, U.S. manufacturers are installing Computer Integrated Manufacturing (CIM) systems. A Flexible Manufacturing System (FMS) is an important component of CIM.

A typical FMS consists of a group of Numerical Control (NC) machine tools connected by an automated material handling system (MHS) under the guidance of a central supervisory computer. These systems emulate the flexibility of job shops while retaining the efficiency of dedicated production lines. The versatility of NC machines enables the system to react quickly and economically to changing requirements. These systems increase productivity by reducing inventory and throughput time. As shown in Figure 1.1, flexible manufacturing systems have been developed to serve the middle ground of batch manufacturing where part variety is too low for dedicated processes but too high for stand alone machine tools. Chang, Wysk, and Wang (1991) have found that today over 90% of production is manufactured in lots of less than 50 parts.

FMS concepts are also used in a variety of other automated processes. These include: assembly, metal forming, painting, and sheet metal operations. Barash (1978) found that the number of flexible manufacturing systems is growing at a rapid rate (estimated to be 5,000 by the year 2000). The actual number of flexible manufacturing systems installed worldwide as of 1990 are at least 1200 (Ayers et al. 1991). These numbers are expected to double every two or three years in the future.

1

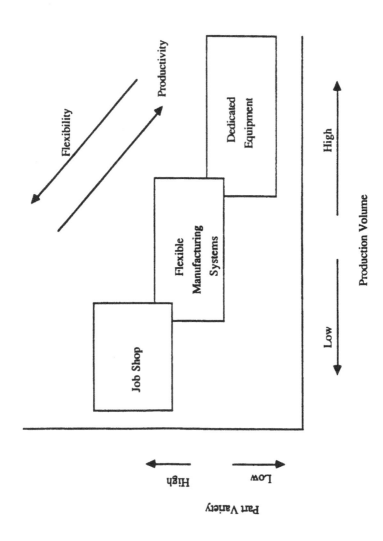

Figure 1.1: Production Systems Application Areas

Currently, there isn't any universally accepted definition of an FMS. Several studies have defined it in different ways. But, the definition of an FMS should answer two questions: (1) What is FMS? and (2) What can it do? That is, the definition should capture its salient features. Thus, this book defines an FMS as:

A flexible manufacturing system is an integrated computer controlled complex of numerically controlled machine tools, automated material and tool handling devices that, with a minimum of manual intervention and short change over time, can process any product belonging to certain specified families of products within its stated capacity and to a predetermined schedule.

Section 1.2 describes a generic FMS. Section 1.3 presents FMS problems. Section 1.4 presents the scope and contributions of this study. Section 1.5 presents the problem setting. Section 1.6 provides the organization of this book.

1.2 DESCRIPTION OF A GENERIC FMS

A typical flexible manufacturing system is shown in Figure 1.2. It consists of a group of machine tools and work stations that are joined by an automated material handling system. All parts of the system operate under computer control. The incoming raw material is fixtured onto pallets at the load/unload station. Each individual palletized workpiece is automatically sent to the required work stations in the sequence appropriate for its processing. The sequence of operations may be different for each part in the system at any one time. In properly designed systems, the holding queues are seldom empty. There is usually a workpiece waiting for processing when a machine becomes idle. Provisions are made for automatic rerouting of parts if a given workstation becomes unavailable or overloaded.

The FMS control computer (CC) keeps track of the status of every part and machine in the system. The CC continually attempts to achieve the production targets for each part type and keeps all machines busy. In dispatching part types to the system, the control computer selects those parts which are required and for which there

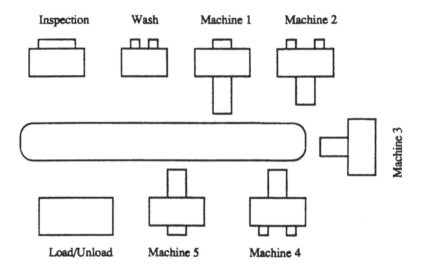

Figure 1.2: A Generic Flexible Manufacturing System.

are available fixtures/pallets and machines. The computer then signals the loader to mount a workpiece on a pallet. The loader then enters the part number and pallet code into the computer terminal. The computer then sends a transporter to the loading station to move the pallet to the machine.

The control computer actuates the transfer mechanism to shift the pallet into the queue, freeing the transporter. Once the machining is completed, the part is removed. A part from the queue is then loaded onto the machine, and the corresponding NC part program is downloaded to the machine controller. Machining then begins on the new part. Once finished, a part waits for a free transporter to carry it to the next destination. If the next destination is unavailable, the computer checks its files for alternate destinations. If an alternate destination exists, the computer decides if conditions on the FMS (backlog, availability, lateness) warrant sending the part to the alternate destination. If it doesn't, the part either circulates around the system on the transporter until the primary destination becomes available, or the transporter unloads it at some intermediate storage queue. It will then retrieve the part when the primary destination becomes available. The last destination of the workpiece is the loading station, which also serves as the unloading station.

The computer controls the cycle described above for all parts and for all machines in the system. It performs the scheduling, dispatching, and traffic coordination functions for the FMS. The CC also monitors tool breakages, tool life, and tool replacements. It also collects statistics and other manufacturing information from each station for reporting purposes.

1.3 THE FMS PROBLEMS

The previous section underlines the complexity involved in the smooth operation of an FMS. For smooth operation of an FMS, it is necessary that the problems involved in the selection stage and operation stage of an FMS are addressed properly. Accordingly, Kusiak (1985) found that two groups of problems need to be addressed once a decision to acquire an FMS is made. They are: (1) design problems, and (2) operational problems. The first group is concerned with the optimal selection of the FMS components. The second group of problems is concerned with the optimal utilization of the FMS.

FMS design problems are related to the decisions that must be made before the installation of an FMS. These decisions include: (1) the selection of parts to be made, (2) the selection of appropriate machine tools, (3) the selection of the material handling system, (4) the computer system configuration, (5) the process design of each part, and (6) the evaluation of different layouts. In this book, operational problems whose solutions affect the efficiency of FMS performance are addressed. Consequently, the above design problems are not discussed.

FMS operational problems involve production planning and scheduling. Stecke (1983) found that production planning in an FMS is more difficult than in assembly lines or job shops because (1) each machine is versatile and is capable of performing different operations; (2) the system can process several different part types simultaneously; and (3) each part may have more than one route in the system.

The decisions involving setting-up of an FMS prior to production are very complex. To alleviate the complexity, Stecke (1983) disaggregated the system planning problem into five sub-problems: part grouping, machine loading, part routing, machine grouping, and production ratio setting. These problems are also referred as pre-release problems. In subsequent studies, each sub-problem was analyzed in isolation. However, it was then shown that the solution of each of the disaggregated sub-problems can lead to an infeasible solution to the total system planning problem.

Drawbacks of the Current Studies

Although the number of flexible manufacturing systems is growing at a rapid rate, proper planning procedures which efficiently utilize these systems have not yet been developed. This observation provides the impetus for this book. In this study, a planning procedure which links various planning sub-problems is developed and an integrated solution procedure is outlined.

Further, prior studies have not analyzed the impact of FMS hardware characteristics and various operating policies on FMS performance. Two important hardware constraints that are included in this study are: (1) machine flexibility, and (2) tool magazine capacity.

Two operating policies that are compared are the maximum production rate policy and the minimum cost policy. The maximum production rate policy is more popular in research studies whereas, the minimum cost policy developed in this book is a surrogate for the needs expressed by the FMS users.

Machine flexibility is built into the system when machines are selected at the design stage. Machine flexibility is the ability of a machine to process an operation (Browne et al., 1984). Two sizes of tool magazines are considered: finite or infinite. The latter is consistent with continuous tool delivery systems or automatic tool interchange (ATI) systems. The infinite tool magazine capacity is that capacity which does not require part grouping. In other words, all required parts can be produced simultaneously. Inclusion of the fore mentioned considerations will not only help FMS managers to better plan and operate an FMS but will also aid management in the design and selection of FMS components.

One of the measures of FMS performance that is used in this study is the flexibility. Several authors, including Hutchinson and Sinha (1989), have found that the lack of quantifiable flexibility measures impedes the justification for an FMS. Although there are enough studies describing various types of flexibilities, studies demonstrating the measurement and application of flexibility are lacking. In this book, operational flexibility measures are developed and used in evaluating production policies and assessing the impact of machine flexibility on FMS performance.

1.4 SCOPE AND CONTRIBUTIONS OF THE STUDY

A detailed discussion of production planning and scheduling is beyond the scope of this book. The specific operational problems studied in this book are the machine loading problem, the part routing problem, and the part grouping problem. The machine loading problem is concerned with the allocation of operations and related tooling among machines subject to capacity constraints. The part routing problem is the selection of route(s) for each part subject to the capacity of the machines. The part grouping problem occurs when all parts cannot be processed simultaneously. A subset of parts is then selected for concurrent production.

This book takes a holistic approach to production planning problems. Specifically, it undertakes a comprehensive study dealing with the effects of machine flexibility, tool magazine capacity, varying production demands, and different operating policies on the production planning problems: part grouping, part routing, and machine loading. Performance measures such as FMS flexibility, makespan, and inventory, are used in evaluating the effects. Three measures of FMS flexibility: actual routing flexibility, potential routing flexibility, and capacity flexibility are defined and operationalized.

Two operating policies are used in the development of loading and routing models. One model incorporates the needs of the FMS users: due-date satisfaction, low inventory holdings, and efficient system utilization, and the other reflects the popular maximize production rate objective widely prevalent in the research literature. The policy developed to reflect the needs of the FMS users is termed minimum cost policy. Simulation studies involving 320 replications of short run production requirements for 32 FMS environments provide important insights into the operation of an FMS. The results show that the minimum cost policy results in significantly lower inventory with higher routing flexibility without statistically affecting the systems capacity, flexibility, or the planned makespan. However, the maximum production rate policy was found to be more sensitive to tool magazine capacity and to variations in production requirements than the minimum cost policy.

In summary, the contributions of this study are:

1.   To develop operational measures of flexibility.
2.   To evaluate loading and routing policies by comparing:
      a) inventory holdings,
      b) FMS flexibility,
      c) FMS utilization, and
      d) the makespan.
3.   To integrate the loading and routing problems. This will reduce computational time and simplify the decision process, because all of the routing combinations do not have to be enumerated explicitly.
4.   To investigate the relationship between machine flexibility and FMS performance.

5. To study the impact of tool magazine capacity on FMS performance.
6. To test the resilience of loading policies to changing production demands.

1.5 THE PROBLEM SETTING

In this study, an FMS is considered to be a component of the firm's manufacturing system. Consequently, the FMS is not studied in isolation as it is important to establish a link between the FMS and its environment. In a study, Kusiak (1986) found that existing studies pertain to machining systems without any integration with the downstream components. That is, the assembly and fabrication systems are ignored. Although a need to integrate the above systems was stressed by Kusiak, few studies have taken this approach. The earliest studies to include downstream components are by Bernardo and Mohamed (1988a, 1988b). In this book, the FMS is considered to have a downstream component and an upstream production component as shown in Figure 1.3. The FMS obtains its raw material from the upstream production component and must satisfy the demand placed on it by the downstream component. This integration of the FMS with its surroundings imposes certain constraints within which it has to operate. First, the FMS should deliver desired parts in required quantities on time to the downstream production component. Second, the FMS should absorb any production disturbances from its upstream component. That is, the FMS should be able to process late jobs and deliver them on time to the downstream production component. In addition, the production requirements placed on the FMS may vary over time, and they must be satisfied in a finite period of time.

The firm's objective is assumed to be the maximization of profits. Because the firm is a price taker in the short run, the objective reduces to minimizing cost. The firm's total cost includes both direct and indirect costs. Direct cost is comprised of production cost and inventory cost. Indirect cost comprises fixed cost and overhead cost. In the short run, the production cost per unit and the indirect costs are fixed. Since the FMS must satisfy its production requirements, short run profit can be maximized by minimizing inventory costs. In this

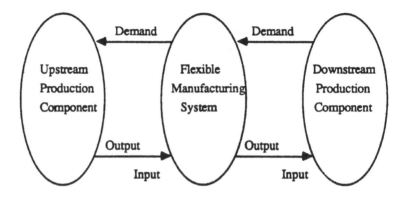

Figure 1.3: An Integrated Manufacturing System.

study, meeting demand at minimum cost is considered as the primary objective. This is consistent with the firm's long run goal of profit maximization and, also agrees with the needs expressed by the FMS users.

In the beginning of the planning horizon, two problems arise: (1) the determination of production requirements, and (2) the route that each part should take.

The first problem is concerned with the determination of part types and the quantity of each part type to produce. This information is an input to the FMS loading problem. As suggested by Nof and Solberg (1980), this problem can be solved by using the information contained in the Master Production Schedule (MPS). The demand for various final products is contained in the MPS. Each final product requires several part types that are produced in the FMS. Consequently, the production requirements placed on the FMS can be calculated from the MPS. This backward translation of the final products' demands yields the production requirements for the FMS.

The second problem that arises is the part routing problem. To determine the route a part type will take, the available routes must first be determined. That is, the tools must be assigned. Following Hutchinson (1977) and Nof et al. (1979), part grouping is only done if there is not enough tool capacity to produce concurrently the FMS demand requirements.

The specific problem analyzed in this book is: given an existing FMS with its production requirements, how should resources be assigned to minimize costs? To answer this question, the following decisions are necessary:

Loading: this decision is concerned with the allocation of operations and related tooling among machines subject to capacity constraints.

Routing: this decision is concerned with the selection of routes for the production of each part type from the available routes subject to machine capacity constraints.

Part Grouping: this decision is concerned with the grouping of part types for concurrent production between tool change-overs if it is not possible to process all of the required part types simultaneously.

The following assumptions are made while addressing the above three problems.

1. The FMS manufactures only those parts which are required by the MPS.
2. The MPS is frozen in the short run. Consequently, rolling horizons will not be analyzed.
3. The FMS is composed of several machines. The machines are non-uniform, that is, a particular operation has different processing times on different machines.
4. The required tools and processing times can be obtained from the process charts.
5. The processing times are assumed to be deterministic.
6. The production can be performed on one part type or a group of part types concurrently.
7. The set-up times are negligible.
8. The long run objective of the firm is to maximize profits.

1.6 OUTLINE OF THE BOOK

This book consists of seven chapters. The following is a brief overview of each chapter.

In this chapter, "Introduction to Flexible Manufacturing Systems," a generic flexible manufacturing system and its planning problems were discussed. The necessity to integrate FMS with its environment was brought into focus. The problems addressed in this book were given along with the scope and contribution of this study.

Chapter 2, "Flexibility," reviews current studies on flexibility. Inconsistencies in the definitions and classifications that exist in the current studies are revealed and a framework for flexibility is suggested. Measures for operational flexibility are developed.

Chapter 3, "Literature Review," provides a detailed literature survey of the planning problems addressed in this book. The specific problems addressed are: (1) machine loading, (2) part routing, and (3) part grouping.

Chapter 4, "Model Formulation," addresses the complexity of production planning in FMS and develops a hierarchical solution procedure to alleviate the complexity. The hierarchy synthesizes and provides a framework for the formulation of mathematical models for the loading, routing and part grouping problems.

Chapter 5, "Development of Hypotheses," deals with the derivation of hypotheses related to planning policies and FMS hardware constraints. Also, experimental design and performance measures are described.

Chapter 6, "Results and Discussions," presents both the results of the hypotheses test and additional findings.

Chapter 7, "Research Implications," provides the managerial implications of the study and lays the directions for future studies.

In addition there are four appendices. Appendix A contains numerical results of simulation. Appendix B presents a fortran code for determining the necessity for part grouping. Appendix C provides mathematical formulation for the determination of capacity flexibility. Appendix D presents a fortran code for the calculation of routing flexibility.

II

Flexibility

All flexible manufacturing systems possess flexibility. This innate flexibility is due to the hardware (such as machines, robots, etc.,) that FMS contains. Although there is built-in flexibility, it is imperative to exploit flexibility to gain competitive advantage by efficiently operating an FMS. Several studies have found that the ways in which flexible manufacturing systems are operated have not fully exploited their flexibility at least as seen in the U.S. and Europe.

The operating decisions such as loading decisions greatly affect FMS flexibility. For example, Stecke and Solberg (1981b) report that the conventional method of assigning an operation to only one machine does not fully utilize the flexibility of the FMS. On the other hand, assigning an operation to multiple machines exhibits more flexibility since any random occurrence of a machine or tool failure will not greatly affect FMS operations. Thus, the loading decision, which assigns operations to machines or groups of work centers, affects FMS flexibility.

The preceding discussions suggest that an FMS possess inherent flexibility and, operating decisions made can exploit it or not. In addition, the amount of flexibility built into the FMS limits the degree to which it can be used. The built-in flexibility (machine flexibility) is an input parameter in this study. Also, since flexibility is used as a performance measure, this study considers two types: routing flexibility, and capacity flexibility. Measures for all three types of flexibility are developed in this chapter.

Section 2.1 discusses the complexity and diversity that exist in studies on flexibility. Section 2.2 develops a framework for flexibility based on relationship to decision making; also, it reviews studies on measurement of flexibility. Section 2.3 discusses the importance of a new direction, applied focus, on flexibility. Section 2.4 develops

15

measurements for machine flexibility, routing flexibility, and capacity flexibility. Finally, this chapter's summary is given in Section 2.5.

2.1 A REVIEW OF FLEXIBILITY

Cox (1989), in a study of manufacturing strategies, reports that firms rank flexibility behind productivity, delivery, and quality in importance for competitiveness. However, flexibility was ranked first in the size of the strategic gap. That is, the difference between current capability and future flexibility needs is perceived to be the largest area for improvement. Although productivity, delivery, quality, and flexibility are critical measures of total manufacturing performance, flexibility is not considered a primary objective. Cox attributes this discrepancy to two factors: (1) productivity, delivery, and quality are well understood and can be translated into comprehensible units such as dollar amounts, and (2) the concept of flexibility is new, with no acceptable measurement, and consequently is treated on an abstract basis rather than on a concrete basis. This latter point becomes evident in the following discussions.

A comprehensive review of the literature on flexibility was first given by Mandelbaum (1978). He describes flexibility as the ability to respond effectively to changing circumstances. Carter (1986) defines flexibility as "Flexibility is a collection of properties of a manufacturing system that support changes in production activities or capabilities."

Flexibility has been defined in different ways by different academics. One consensus is that the flexibility is multi-dimensional. To get a good perception of flexibility, it was broken down into various types. The diversity and conflict that exist in the definitions of various types of flexibilities are evident in the works of Browne et al. (1984), Gupta and Goyal (1989), Carter (1986), Kumar (1986), Sethi and Sethi (1990), Swamidass (1988), Bernardo and Mohamed (1992), Suarez et al. (1991), Slack (1988), and Gerwin (1993) to name a few. Sethi and Sethi (1990), and Gupta and Goyal (1989) provide excellent reviews on various flexibility types that exist in the current studies.

Different types of flexibility

The concept of flexibility is generally used loosely, but several studies have attempted to describe different types of flexibilities. Besides, current definitions are not precise and the same concept is given different names in different studies. These observations become readily apparent in the following discussions. Several studies are discussed; but first, eight types of flexibilities of Browne et al. (1984) are given.

Machine Flexibility: It refers to the ease of making changes to produce a given set of part types. This flexibility can be attained by (a) technological progress, (b) delivery of part and required tooling together to the machine tool, and (c) proper operation assignment that minimizes tool changes. This flexibility can be measured as a time for replacement of worn or broken tools, time to mount fixtures, tool change time for different production runs, etc.

Process Flexibility: It is the ability to produce a given set of part types, possibly made of different materials, in several ways. This flexibility is the same as *job flexibility* of Buzacott (1982), *mix flexibility* of Gerwin (1982), and *adequacy flexibility* of Zelenovic (1982). This flexibility can be measured by the number of different part types that can simultaneously be produced without using batches. This flexibility can be attained by having (a) machine flexibility, and (b) multi-purpose, adaptable, CNC machining centers.

Product Flexibility: Product flexibility is the capability to change product mix rapidly and inexpensively. This flexibility is similar to *action flexibility* of Mandelbaum (1978), *design change flexibility* of Gerwin (1982), and *adaptation flexibility* of Zelenovic (1982). This flexibility can be measured as the time required to change from one product mix to another. Product flexibility can be attained through (a) good automated planning and a control mechanism and (b) machine flexibility.

Routing Flexibility: It is the ability to continue to process jobs on alternate routes/alternate machines in case of a breakdown. This flexibility can be measured by the robustness of FMS when a breakdown occurs. Routing flexibility can be attained by (a) pooling machines into groups, (b) duplicating operational assignments, and (c) providing alternate tools.

Volume Flexibility: Volume flexibility is the ability of an FMS to operate profitably at all volume levels. A higher level of automation increases this flexibility through reduced set-up costs and direct labor costs. This flexibility can be measured by how small the volumes can be for all part types with the system still being run profitably. The lower the volume, the more volume flexible the system is. This flexibility can be attained through machine and routing flexibilities.

Expansion Flexibility: It is the capability of modularly building and expanding a system easily if needed; that is, the capability to increase the capacity or to change the product envelope. This flexibility can be attained by having (a) a non-dedicated, non-process driven layout, (b) routing flexibility, (c) AGV's, and (d) modular machining cells.

Operation Flexibility: Operation flexibility is the ability to interchange the ordering of several operations that have no precedence requirements for each part type. Instead of a fixed sequence for operations, keeping the routes open increases this flexibility.

Production Flexibility: Product flexibility is the universe of part types the system can produce. This flexibility is measured by the level of technology and all other previously discussed flexibilities.

Some flexibilities discussed thus far are dependent, which implies a hierarchy of flexibility types (Sethi and Sethi 1990, Chung and Chen 1990). The goals determine the key flexibilities to be designed into the manufacturing system. Product, operation, and process flexibilities depend on machine flexibility. Volume and expansion flexibilities depend on routing flexibility. However, production flexibility depends on all above flexibilities.

The classification of Browne et al. (1984) does not consider the capabilities of the other components of FMS: namely, the material handling system and the computer system configuration. Nevertheless, Kusiak (1986) includes them in his classification of four types of flexibility:

Flexible Manufacturing Module (FMM) Flexibility: This is measured by the number of parts that can be processed on the FMM, and this is similar to the *production flexibility* of Browne et al. (1984).

Material Handling System (MHS) Flexibility: This is concerned with the ability of the MHS to handle different parts on a number of different routes.

Computer System Flexibility: This is measured by its adaptability to the changing functions.

Organizational Flexibility: Kusiak proposes that to attain organizational flexibility, it is essential to attain the following flexibilities. The flexibilities and their descriptions are:

Job Flexibility is the mix of parts that the FMS can process, and this is the same as the *job flexibility* of Buzacott (1982).

Scheduling Flexibility is measured by the number of routes along which a job can be manufactured, and this is the same as the *routing flexibility* of Browne et al. (1984).

Short-term Flexibility is measured by the change-over cost between known production programs, and this is the same as the *product flexibility* of Browne et al. (1984).

Long-term Flexibility is measured by the set-up cost of the new production tasks due to change in the production programs, and this is the same as the *expansion flexibility* of Browne et al. (1984).

2.2 A FRAMEWORK FOR FLEXIBILITY

Swamidass (1988) has attributed the problem of understanding flexibility to three underlining problems: (1) the scope of flexibility related terms used by various authors overlap, (2) some flexibility terms are aggregates of other flexibility terms, and (3) identical flexibility terms used by various authors do not necessarily have the same meaning. The discussions of Section 2.1 and a look at Table 2.1 readily convey that Swamidass was correct in his conclusions.

Authors	Operational Flexibility		Design Flexibility					
	Product Flexibility	Routing Flexibility	Process Flexibility	Machine Flexibility	Operation Flexibility	Expansion Flexibility	Volume Flexibility	Production Flexibility
Browne et al. [1984]	Product Flexibility	Routing Flexibility	Process Flexibility	Machine Flexibility	Operation Flexibility	Expansion Flexibility	Volume Flexibility	Production Flexibility
Buzacott [1982]			Job Flexibility	Machine Flexibility				
Kusiak [1986]	Short-term Flexibility	Scheduling Flexibility	Job Flexibility			Long-term Flexibility		FMM Flexibility
Gerwin [1982]	Design Change Flexibility		Mix Flexibility					
Mandelbaum [1978]	Action Flexibility	State Flexibility						
Warnecke and Steinhilper [1982]	Short-term Flexibility					Long-term Flexibility		
Zelenovic [1982]	Adaptation Flexibility		Adequacy Flexibility					
Son & Park [1987]	Product * Flexibility		Process * Flexibility	Machine * Flexibility				
Kumar [1986]					Operation* Flexibility			

Table 2.1 : Inconsistencies in the Nomenclature of Various Types of Flexibility.
(* means measures are provided).

Relationship to Decision Making

To alleviate the difficulties cited by Swamidass, it is necessary to study flexibility types in view of changes with which they are associated. A categorization of the existing studies on flexibility based on long-term and short-term changes is given in Table 2.1. The classification also can be based on qualitative vs. quantitative measures, and theoretical vs. non-theoretical measures (see Gupta and Goyal 1989).

In Table 2.1, flexibility types defined in major studies are categorized according to their relationship to the decision making situation that they affect. These classifications, *operational flexibility* and *design flexibility*, result from viewing the management problems that occur in an FMS as tactical or strategic problems. Each row of Table 1 refers to the flexibility types used by authors listed in column 1. All of the flexibility terms that appear in one column are terms that are used by the various authors to refer to the same general flexibility concept.

Kumar (1986) agrees with Swamidass (1988) that different studies label same flexibility concepts differently and, sometimes use the same name to denote different concepts. Unfortunately, beyond confusing the concept of flexibility, current studies do not suggest an explicit analytical framework for the understanding of flexibility. The need to explicitly consider flexibility makes it necessary to break it into various types and develop measures for each type.

Before measures can be developed, it is necessary to identify those flexibilities which have relationships with various decisions. This can be achieved by classifying the types of flexibilities according to their impact with long-term and short-term decisions. The long-term decisions are strategic decisions and involve substantial investments. The short-term decisions are involved with the operation of FMS. In this study, flexibility associated with strategic decisions is called *Design Flexibility* and the flexibility associated with short-term is called *Operational Flexibility.*

Design flexibility is built into the FMS at the design stage. This flexibility is predominantly technology based and is concerned with the built in resources flexibility. To enhance this flexibility, the machines, material handling, automatic tool changing, etc., are made more versatile, more complex, and are provided with more sophisticated controls.

Operational flexibility is concerned with the use of FMS. The loading and routing decisions affect this flexibility. For example, allowing a part to take only one route lowers the routing flexibility. Some machines may be under-utilized, while others are congested. This may restrict the part mix, thus affecting the product flexibility. Product flexibility of Browne et al. (1984) involves changing over from one part mix to another. Since due dates have to be met in this study, a sudden demand for a different part type can be satisfied only if there is enough capacity. Flexibility that deals with change in part mix, or copes with additional demand for the same part mix, or satisfies demand for a new part, is called *Capacity Flexibility.* Hence, for an efficient utilization of FMS, both routing flexibility and capacity flexibility are necessary.

Since this book focusses on the operational problems, relevant flexibility that will be addressed is operational flexibility. Design flexibility (specifically, machine flexibility) is assumed to be fixed for a given FMS. To study the relationship between operational decisions and operational flexibility, it is necessary to develop measure for flexibility. This will help managers to use FMS more efficiently. Existing studies lack this perspective. The following section deals with current studies on the measurement of flexibility.

Existing Flexibility Measures

The flexibilities so far discussed are not distinct and need precise definitions, and this will help in developing proper procedures for their measurements. In recent years, studies on the measurement of flexibility types have appeared, but they have failed to yield insights into their applications. Chatterjee et al. (1984), Zelenovic (1982), and Gustavsson (1984) among others, have suggested measures for flexibility based on physical characteristics. Flexibility does not come from physical characteristics alone but is a result of a combination of factors like operating policies, physical characteristics, and management practices (Gupta and Buzacott 1989).

Kusiak (1986) defines a unit flexibility as a ratio of the overall FMS flexibility to the number of machines in the FMS. But how to measure this overall FMS flexibility is not given. According to

Gustavsson (1984), machine flexibility is measured as the ratio of the investment's residual value for the next product model to the original investment, i.e., an index between 0 and 1. Product flexibility is measured as the residual value of the old model to the new model divided by the original value for the old model.

Primerose (1984) measures the FMS flexibility as the ratio of the number of arcs of a particular FMS to the number of arcs in an *ideal* FMS with the same number of machines. Here the arcs represent the routes for parts, and an *ideal* FMS contains machines that are capable of executing any operation.

Son and Park (1987) define measurements for machine, product, and process flexibilities in dollar terms. The measures are ratios of cost of output to the idle cost of the equipment, set-up cost, and waiting time cost, respectively. They measure the demand flexibility as a ratio of output in cost units to the inventory costs of finished products and raw materials.

Chatterjee et al. (1986) develop a general framework to quantify flexibility in manufacturing systems. They group machines into module centers; each module has its own material handling system (MHS), and they are connected to each other by another MHS. A comprehensive module with respect to a part is one for which routing can be accomplished within the center. Two flexibility measures are defined as (a) the ratio of the number of comprehensive module centers for a part to the total number of comprehensive module centers, and (b) the ratio of the number of comprehensive module centers for a part to the number of parts which have comprehensive module centers.

The drawback with the cost measurements is that the cost structure may be unique to each firm, and hence a flexibility value for the same FMS may be different in different firms. An ideal FMS may not exist, making measurement suggested by Primerose (1984) inapplicable. If the FMS cannot be ordered into module centers, the measure suggested by Chatterjee et al. (1986) yields a ratio of zero to zero, which does not exist.

There are numerous other attempts to quantify flexibility. For example, Upton and Barash (1988), and Brill and Mandelbaum (1989, 1990) have also expressed problems associated with measuring flexibility. Sethi and Sethi (1990) have provided a detailed review of existing measures. Kumar and Kumar (1988) and Gupta and Goyal

(1989) attempted to categorize various flexibility measures into six types of approaches: economic consequence, performance criteria, multi-dimensional approaches, petri-net approaches, information theoretic approaches, and decision theoretic approaches. They argued that "... most of these measurements are often constrained in that they submit an incomplete rendition of the measured flexibility type. Most of these measures fail to take job characteristics into consideration and they have not specified units of measurement, while some others are too complex."

Further, none of the flexibilities addressed pertains to operational flexibility. As operational flexibility is achieved by having routing and capacity flexibilities, measures for these two flexibilities are developed later in this chapter.

2.3 A REFOCUS ON FLEXIBILITY

A review of studies on flexibility reveals that it has been broken down into various types differently. Further, these flexibility types have been defined and categorized in various ways. These disparities are due to the complex nature of flexibility. Nonetheless, the vagueness can be resolved by attempting to understand how one type of flexibility interacts with other types of flexibilities.

The present advances made in the theory of flexibility are not sufficient to undertake a comprehensive study dealing with the interactions among all types of flexibilities. However, such a study may be feasible by building blocks between flexibility types gradually. Thus, this study attempts to analyze the effects of machine flexibility on the routing flexibility, capacity flexibility, and other performance measures such as inventory and makespan under different production environments. That is, the impact of long-term decision on the short-term performance of an FMS is studied.

The machine flexibility refers to the types of operations performed without difficulty in switching from one to the other. The routing flexibility is the ability to process parts on alternate routes, and capacity flexibility refers to the percent of average demand that can be satisfied by the system after having met the present production requirements (Bernardo and Mohamed 1992). Operational flexibility is the ability of the FMS to adjust to changes in part-mix, part type demand, and machine failures which can be achieved by having both the routing flexibility and capacity flexibility.

There are abundant studies on FMS design problems, operational problems, and theoretical work on flexibility. However, Gerwin (1993) points that studies on flexibility need to have an applied focus to complement the existing theoretical work. As the three issues (design, operation, and flexibility) are interrelated, an applied focus on flexibility helps in selecting and using operating policies which better utilize FMS flexibility. This study demonstrates this point.

The present study adopts Gerwin's multilevel scheme for flexibility: machine → manufacturing system or cell → plant or multiplant levels. According to his classification, machine flexibility is at the machine level, and routing and capacity flexibilities are at the manufacturing system level. An applied focus should try to establish the degree of effect of one level (e.g., machine flexibility) on the other level (e.g., routing flexibility and capacity flexibility) and explore its sensitivity with respect to FMS operating policies and changing production environments.

As discussed before, flexibility has been defined in different ways by different academics. One consensus is that the flexibility is multi-dimensional. In order to get a good perception of flexibility, researchers broke it down into various types. Although it was necessary to look into the flexibility by each researcher in his own way to expand the knowledge, the future studies should attempt to obliterate the confusion and ambiguities that have resulted from previous studies. It is now necessary to undertake studies which establish relationships between various flexibility types and how the management philosophy adopted in operating FMS affects those flexibilities and their relationships. This is essential as several studies have found that the ways in which FMSs are operated have not fully exploited their flexibility at least as seen in North America and Europe (Jaikumar 1986, Reich 1983, Graham and Rosenthal 1986).

It can be inferred from the North American and European experiences that to fully utilize FMS's potentials (flexibility) a manager should know how to take advantage of long-term benefits in terms of short-term actions. Accordingly, in this study existing flexibility types were classified into design flexibility and operational flexibility based on their impact on long-term and short-term decisions, respectively. The concepts of design flexibility and operational flexibility are the same as *potential flexibility* and *actual flexibility* of Gerwin (1993), respectively. Whatever may be the potential flexibility, it is important to exploit it because: (1) analysis of the discrepancies between potential and actual flexibility can help operations managers evaluate their needs for various types of flexibilities, and (2) managers should not overlook the opportunity to identify and eliminate excess flexibility because having too much flexibility may be uneconomical.

One reason for managers to opt for higher potential flexibility is to increase the manufacturing flexibility. Diverse process capabilities and how organizations use these capabilities contribute to the manufacturing flexibility. Manufacturing flexibility of a production system is the ability of the system to adapt to instability induced by changing environment and process requirements (Swamidass 1988). Instability is introduced into the system by factors such as new product introduction, stochastic production demand, and machine failures.

To remain competitive, Swamidass ascribes three ingredients to manufacturing flexibility: process flexibility, product design flexibility, and infrastructure flexibility. Process and product design flexibilities are built into the system at the design and implementation stages. Infrastructure flexibility, which Ranta (1989) also agrees, is obtained from the business philosophy and other supporting functions such as planning and scheduling, data collection, JIT, etc. The concepts of design and operational flexibilities are consistent with the requirements prescribed by Swamidass. Because the physical system (FMS) has design and operational flexibility, a difference in the operational performance is to be expected. Thus, this study investigates these differences relative to productivity and flexibility.

As one type of flexibility (see Sethi and Sethi 1990 for types of flexibilities) overlaps with the other, or induces the other (machine flexibility → routing flexibility), a firm can simultaneously obtain the effects of different types of flexibility (Noori 1990). However, the firm must decide which type of flexibility is more crucial for its competitiveness before implementing a given level of automation. Any discussion of flexibility must consider the potential connection between the level of technology (design flexibility) and the inherent degree of flexibility (operational flexibility). That is, the relationship between design flexibility and operational flexibility must be considered. The need to explicitly consider flexibility makes it necessary to classify flexibility into various types and define measures for each type.

2.4 DEVELOPMENT OF FLEXIBILITY MEASURES

Researchers need flexibility measures to test theories and operations managers need them for a different purpose-to help make capital investment decisions and determine performance levels (Gerwin 1993). In spite of the need, well-accepted measures are yet to be developed. As discussed before, some authors have quantified flexibility based on counting options (Chatterjee, et al. 1984, Primerose 1984), entropy (Yao 1985, Kumar 1986, Brill and Mandelbaum 1987, 1989), dollar amounts (Gustavsson 1984, Son and Park 1987), or probability and time (Zelenovic 1982). Although Sethi and Sethi (1990) presents an extensive survey of existing flexibility measures, an aggregate measure for overall FMS flexibility has yet to be developed. Given the fact that flexibility is multi-dimensional, an aggregate measure for overall FMS flexibility may have little, or no practical usefulness. Nonetheless, the measure for each flexibility type sheds light on the capability and performance of an FMS.

Machine Flexibility

Machine flexibility is its capability to process as many operation types as possible relative to a desired operations set. Before developing a measure for machine flexibility in a production setting, few definitions are in order. An operation or a task is an activity which changes the present characteristics of a part. For example, a surface milling operation produces a smooth surface. A part may need more than one task (operation) performed on it during its manufacturing. That is, a part i is manufactured by performing a task set T_i. As FMS is designed based on a set of parts it should manufacture, a universal task set, $T = \cup T_i$, is defined to be a set that contains all tasks needed to manufacture all parts. Let τ be a member of task set T.

The machine-task feasibility rating $e(M,\tau)$ indicates whether machine M can perform task τ or not. It is assumed to take on a value of 1 if feasible, 0 otherwise. The machine M capability set relative to reference task set T is defined by $M_{e,T}=\{\tau\in T/e(M,\tau)=1\}$. The machine M capability set is the set of all tasks in reference set T that can be performed by it.

Machine flexibility relative to a task set T

This measure is defined by:

$$F_{M,T} = \frac{|M_{e,T}|}{|T|}$$

The above measure for machine flexibility is different from that given by Brill and Mandelbaum (1989, 1990). The above measure is based on counting options, whereas their measure is based on a weighting scheme. In their scheme the weights are selected by a decision maker, and since weights are subjective, two decision makers may arrive at different values for the same machine. The above measure is independent of any subjective input. Notice that as Σ_τ $e(M,\tau)\le |T|$, $0\le F_{M,T}\le 1$. A value of 1 represents a case of fully flexible machine (100% machine flexibility) capable of doing all tasks of task set T, which is reasonable.

Flexibility of a group of machines relative to task set T

The same definitions as given before are used except that machine M is referred as M^j. Let $G=\{M^1, ..., M^n\}$ be a set of machines forming an FMS. Let $F_{G,T}$ be defined as machine flexibility of FMS.

As before, let $e(M^j,T)$ represent machine-task feasibility rating and has a binary value (0,1). Define task-machine feasibility set relative to a group of machines G as $\tau_{e,G}=\{M^j\in G/e(M^j,\tau)=1\}$. The task-machine feasibility set $\tau_{e,G}$ is the set of all machines that can perform this task.

Then the flexibility of a group of machines relative to a task set T is:

$$F_{G,T} = \frac{\Sigma_\tau F_{G,\tau}}{|T|}$$

where,

$$F_{G,\tau} = \frac{| \tau_{e,G} |}{| G |}$$

Note that $0 \leq F_{G,T} \leq 1$ and $0 \leq F_{G,\tau} \leq 1$. Also, note that $F_{G,T}=1 \Rightarrow F_{G,\tau}=1$ for all τ. This means that each task can be performed by all machines, or each machine is capable of performing all tasks of set $\tau \in T$; this makes FMS fully flexible, which is reasonable.

Although machine flexibility affects overall system performance, past studies have concentrated only on the system throughput (Vinod and Solberg 1985, Buzacott and Shanthikumar 1980, Buzacott and Yao 1986, Dallery and Frein 1986, Bitran and Tirupati 1987). Besides system throughput, the other important determinant of FMS capability is its operational flexibility. Operational flexibility is the ability of the FMS to adjust to changes in part-mix, part type demand, and machine failures (Bernardo and Mohamed 1992).

A flexible manufacturing system should be designed to handle disturbances. These disturbances are introduced through changes in part-mix, part type demand, and machine failures. The ability of an FMS to respond to these disturbances can be captured by routing and capacity flexibilities. Routing flexibility can result from either the assigned routes that a part type actually uses, or the potential routes that result from tool loading. Accordingly, two types of routing flexibilities: actual routing flexibility and potential routing flexibility, exist.

Routing Flexibility

Routing flexibility is the ability of the system to continue producing a given part mix despite internal and/or external disturbances. A part i can be produced from N_i number of routes. However, due to the limited capacity of the machines and other parts competing for the same resources, only a subset of the N_i routes will be assigned to the actual production of part i. These routes are termed production routes for part i, PR_i. If one of the production routes becomes unavailable due to machine failure or other disturbances, another production route could be employed. *Actual Routing Flexibility*, ARF_i, is a measure of the number of existing production routes that could be used. Actual routing flexibility is defined as:

$$ARF_i = 1 - (1 / PR_i)$$

For a transfer line, PR_i is one, yielding $ARF_i = 0$. For a job shop, PR_i would be very large resulting in a routing flexibility that approaches 1. Both results are to be expected.

If the machines are capable and the appropriate tools are assigned, part i can be made on alternate routes that are not currently assigned to make part i. Total available routes (AR_i) include both production routes and alternate routes. By providing alternate routes, the ability of the system to take up production of part i in the event of machine failures on regular routes is enhanced. This type of routing flexibility is termed, *Potential Routing Flexibility*, PRF_i, and is expressed as:

$$PRF_i = 1 - (1 / AR_i)$$

Capacity Flexibility

Besides using routes to adjust for disturbances, capacity can also be used as buffer. In the short run, an FMS faces variable demand for a set of parts. If the quantity demanded in any one time period is increased, the additional demand could be met if additional capacity is available for the part(s) with altered demand. *Capacity Flexibility*, CF_i, is defined as the ability of the system to respond to unanticipated demand for part i. Clearly, for a given tool assignment, there is a maximum quantity that can be made of part i. The higher the maximum quantity of a part that can be produced relative to its average or expected demand, the more capacity flexibility exists in a given tool assignment. The maximum quantity that can be produced of a part is composed of the sum of quantities that are produced and the quantity that could be made. Capacity flexibility for part i can be measured as;

$$CF_i = \frac{\text{\# of extra units of part } i \text{ that can be made from all routes}}{\text{Average demand of part } i}$$

CF_i indicates the additional proportion of average demand for part i the system can produce under existing operating conditions. The interpretation of $CF_i = 0$ means that the available capacity of the system has been completely used in satisfying the production requirements and, there is no capacity left to meet contingencies like a surge in demand or machine breakdowns. Hence, the system is inflexible in terms of reacting to any emergency request. $CF_i > 0$ is always preferable.

In all three measures, flexibility is expressed with respect to a part type. To determine the aggregate flexibility of the FMS for each flexibility measure, the above quantities must be summed over all part types. The sum is weighted with respect to the percent of total quantity demanded in each period. The aggregate measures for the above flexibility types are given in Figure 2.1.

The above aggregate flexibility measures represent the average ability of the system to handle internal and external disturbances given the production plan. It should be noted that these measures are sensitivity measures in that they represent the bounds on the disturbances beyond which the system would not be able to respond. For example, an aggregate capacity flexibility of 0.3 means that after satisfying the average demand imposed, the FMS still has enough capacity to meet an extra 30% of the average demand. This extra demand may come from a surge in production requirements, or machine failures. In the case of machine failures, the above implication means that the FMS can satisfy the given production requirements only if the capacity lost due to machine failures is less than or equal to 30%. Hence, the higher the flexibility measures are, the larger are the disturbances the system can handle.

2.5 SUMMARY

In this chapter, studies on flexibility were reviewed. The complex nature of flexibility was demonstrated through the disagreements that exists in the classification and categorization of various types of flexibilities. As a step toward removing ambiguity, a framework for classifying various flexibility types was suggested. The need for an applied focus to flexibility, a departure from theoretical work, was demonstrated. Measures for flexibility were then developed to aid in implementing the new focus to flexibility.

$$ARF_{it} = 1 - \frac{1}{PR_{it}}$$

$$PRF_{it} = 1 - \frac{1}{AR_{it}}$$

$$CF_{it} = \frac{\textit{extra units of part i that can be made from all routes}}{\textit{Average Demand of part i}}$$

$$FMS\ ARF = \sum_{t} \frac{\sum_{i} D_{it}}{\sum_{t}\sum_{i} D_{it}} \sum_{i} ARF_{it} \frac{D_{it}}{\sum_{i} D_{it}}$$

$$FMS\ PRF = \sum_{t} \frac{\sum_{i} D_{it}}{\sum_{t}\sum_{i} D_{it}} \sum_{i} PRF_{it} \frac{D_{it}}{\sum_{i} D_{it}}$$

$$FMS\ CF = \sum_{t} \frac{\sum_{i} D_{it}}{\sum_{t}\sum_{i} D_{it}} \sum_{i} CF_{it} \frac{D_{it}}{\sum_{i} D_{it}}$$

where :

PR_i = *Production Routes for part i in period t*

AR_i = *Available Routes for part i in period t*

ARF = *Actual Routing Flexibility*

PRF = *Potential Routing Flexibility*

CF = *Capacity Flexibility*

Figure 2.1: Aggregate Flexibility Measures.

III

Literature Review

In Chapter I, it was noted that to pursue the firm's goals, it is critical to integrate FMS with its environment. To exploit a flexible manufacturing system's full capability it is necessary to develop a good planning procedure which deals with the planning problems properly. This chapter addresses this issue in detail. Also, this chapter presents reviews of the existing studies pertaining to planning problems dealt in this study. The insights gained from these reviews form the focus of this book. Specifically, this book addresses the following planning problems: machine loading, part routing, and part grouping.

The layout of this chapter is as follows: In Section 3.1, a review of studies pertaining to planning hierarchies is addressed. Planning hierarchies provide relationships between various planning problems. A review of studies dealing with the part grouping problem and their limitations is discussed in Section 3.2. Similar reviews of the studies on the FMS loading problem and the routing problem are presented in Section 3.3 and Section 3.4, respectively. It will be shown that the existing studies on the loading and routing problems do not satisfy the needs of the FMS users. Finally, a summary is given in Section 3.5.

3.1 PLANNING HIERARCHY

Various studies have proposed hierarchies with design decisions at the top level and system operation decisions at the lower levels (e.g., Gershwin et al. 1986, Suri and Whitney 1984). Although there seems to be consensus in placing design decisions at the top level, they seem to vary at other levels where decisions regarding FMS

33

operations are made. This is due to the differences in their approaches to the FMS operations problem and the complexity of this problem.

Planning hierarchies have been proposed for the dynamic production environment (e.g., Hildebrant 1980, Kimemia and Gershwin 1984) as well as in static production environment (e.g., Stecke 1984, Kusiak 1986). In a dynamic environment the system status is known at all times. Jobs are routed to the first available machine, even though that may not be the best decision; because there could be another machine that is best suited to perform the work.

In a static environment, the system status is not considered; and schedules are made off-line often resulting in infeasible schedules when implemented. A combination of both approaches will take advantage of each approach and hence may improve the system performance.

Hierarchies for Dynamic Environment

Hildebrant (1980) was the first to consider the overall FMS production planning and control problems. He proposed the following hierarchy:

Level 1. Find the mix of jobs and machine-operation assignment for each job under all possible combinations of working and failed machines in order to minimize the time to achieve the production target.

Level 2. Find the sequence of jobs entering the system in each failure condition to maximize the average production rate.

Level 3. Find for each job its input time and its next operation in each failure condition in order to minimize the delay in the system.

Although machine breakdowns are considered, the assumption that the system is in equilibrium without a transient phase is questionable. In reality a system may take longer to reach equilibrium.

In contrast to Hildebrant's work, which links the FMS with its environment by a production target, Kimemia (1982) decouples the FMS by having a downstream buffer on its output side and a controller on its input side. The input controller implements the decisions from the Master Production Plan. The hierarchy has the following structure:

Flow Control. Determine the production rate for each job considering inventory levels at the downstream buffer, machine reliability information, and changes in production requirement.

Routing Control. With throughput derived from the flow control level determine the optimal routing of jobs to minimize the congestion in the system.

Sequence Control. With the objective of maintaining the throughput and routing decisions from the upper levels determine the next operation of internal jobs, sequence and release time of an external job into the system.

Based on the assumption of modeling discrete part movements as a continuous flow, the optimal policy is shown to be a feedback control rule which is piece-wise constant. That is, the flow controller tends to maintain a constant production rate over short intervals. The inverse of this interval is taken for each job as its release time (loading interval) into the system.

In view of the capital intensive nature of FMS's, it is imperative to design and operate them as efficiently as possible. To this effect, Suri and Whitney (1984) proposed and developed a decision support system based on the following decision hierarchy:

Long Term. Decisions regarding product mix, system configuration and hardware selection are made. Provision for system modification or expansion is considered.

Medium Term. Decisions regarding batching of parts and balancing of work in each batch are made to minimize total flow time and maximize the average machines utilization.

Short Term. Decisions concerning the real time control of FMS are made. This includes which part to be introduced next, sequence of operations, scheduling of material handling system, and reaction to production interruptions such as machine and tool failures.

In view of the complexity of the FMS and potential diversity of part routings and variations in processing times, Buzacott and Shanthikumar (1980) propose control of the system at three levels:

Pre-release Planning. Determine the parts for processing, their operation sequence, and operation processing times.

Input Control. Determine the sequence and release of jobs to the system.

Operational Control. Determine the loading assignment. If a number of alternatives exist, resolve the conflict between the choice of machines considering their functional status.

Hierarchies for Static Environment

The above hierarchies deal with decision making under dynamic conditions. Kusiak (1986) proposes the following hierarchy suitable under static production environment:

Level 4. This concerns with aggregate planning. Products are grouped into product types; and with necessary modifications, a model similar to Bitran et al. (1981, 1982) can be used.

Level 3. This concerns with resource grouping. Parts are grouped into families, and machines are grouped into Flexible Manufacturing Cells (FMC). Classification and coding systems can be used to group parts (Kusiak 1984), or Group Technology approaches can be used (Chakravarty and Shtub 1984).

Level 2. This concerns with disaggregation. The families are optimally loaded onto FMC's. Batching of parts is done because of the limited tool holding capacities of the machines.

Level 1. At this level, scheduling of material handling system, pallets and fixtures, tools, and robots to the individual machines is executed.

In a study, Stecke (1984) classifies FMS problems into four categories: (1) *Design,* (2) *Planning,* (3) *Scheduling,* and (4) *Control.* Before the system can begin to produce, the system set-up problem must be solved. She identifies the following five short-term problems that need to be solved sequentially or simultaneously for a solution to FMS planning problem.

Machine grouping. Partition the machines into machine groups in such a way that each machine in a particular group is able to perform the same set of operations.

Resource grouping. Allocate the limited number of pallets and fixtures of each type among the selected part types.

Production ratio. Determine the relative ratios at which the subset of part types selected for concurrent processing will be produced.

Machine loading. Allocate the operations and required tools of the selected part types among the machine groups subject to technological and capacity constraints of the FMS.

Part type selection. From a set of part types that have production requirements, determine a subset (part group) for immediate and concurrent processing.

Although Kusiak (1986), and Stecke (1984) have proposed the planning sub-problems, they fail to indicate the order or the linkage between those problems.

3.2 PART GROUPING

The part types to be made are determined from customer orders or forecasted demand. There are some constraints that make part grouping an indispensable component of FMS planning problems. The most important one is the limited capacities of machine tool magazines. It restricts the number of tools that can be mounted on the tool magazines and constrains the number of part types that can be processed simultaneously. If tool magazine capacity is big enough to process all part types, then part grouping is not needed.

Another constraint is that tool transfer between machines or central tool storage is not allowed during the time the system is in operation. If the system is equipped with tool transfer devices, the tool magazines virtually have no capacity constraint. Thus, part grouping is not necessary; but a new problem of tool scheduling would arise.

Two assumptions are used to make the part grouping problem easier to solve. First, the part being processed must be completely finished and should not return for further processing. Second, each part type requires a unique set of tools.

Existing studies consider the part grouping problem and machine loading problem independently. A consequence of this is, if part selection yields a set of tools that require more slots than are available; no tool assignment is even possible.

A review of the related work on part selection can be divided into three categories: 1) heuristic approaches, 2) group technology approaches, and 3) mathematical programming.

Heuristic Approaches

A heuristic approach to grouping part types for each batch was suggested by Whitney and Goul (1985). A batch for concurrent production in an FMS can be proposed on the basis of its resource requirements in comparison to aggregate resources available from the system. Whitney and Goul use a sequential decision approach, which is a greedy method. This method tries to maximize an estimated probabilistic performance index, P_s, which is defined as $P_s = \sum_{i \in I'} P_{si}$. I' is the set of parts not yet selected into the batch, and P_{si} is the probability of eventual inclusion of part i in the batch. The procedure sequentially selects a part that will result in the highest P_s from unselected parts. The value of P_{si} is determined taking into consideration the balancing of workload, P_{ti}, the degree of sharing of tools, P_{wi}, and the due date, P_n. P_{si} is defined as $P_{si}=1-P_{ti}(1-P_{wi}(1-P_n))$. P_{wi}, P_{ti}, and P_n are calculated using complicated functions.

However, four drawbacks of this method should be noted: (1) The assumption of independence between parts is wrong, since they are competing for the same resources; (2) If P_{si} is little larger than P_{sj} but has a much larger variance, it is not clear which one should be selected for the batch; (3) The algorithm does not yield a global optimum (Hwang 1986); (4) There is no guarantee that all of the objectives are satisfied.

Another heuristic approach to batching is given by Bastos (1988). His objective function is the maximization of performance index, which takes into account the availability of pallets, routes and processing times. The drawback of his method is the computational intractability for larger size problems due to the increased number of variables and constraints.

Group Technology Approach

Another approach to part grouping is to apply techniques of group technology and cluster analysis. Kusiak (1985) addresses some of the available tools for grouping such as classification and coding schemes. The classification scheme uses coding systems to describe the characteristics of the part based on its geometrical shape and processing needs. The coding systems use digits to characterize a part with each digit representing an attribute. To identify part families, a measure of similarity based on the distance between two parts is taken. The drawback with using this approach is that the distance measure is subjective, and one can obtain different solutions for the same problem.

To overcome the above drawback, the GT research began to group parts and machines simultaneously. This approach uses a part-machine incident matrix instead of a long string of digits. The incident matrix has element $a_{ij} = 1$ if part i can be processed by machine j, else $a_{ij} = 0$. The problem is to cluster all non-zero a_{ij}'s diagonally. This is achieved by the rank order clustering algorithms of King and Nakoranchai (1982). If the form does exist, this algorithm can identify the diagonal block form in O(mnlog(mn)), where m is the number of machines and n is the number of parts. When the form does not exist, adjustment rules based on subjective judgment are used.

GT techniques have proved to be useful in selecting parts at the design stage of FMS (Draper 1984; Hutchinson 1984). However, in the production stage, the machine tools and parts for processing have been fixed; and the problem is to utilize optimally the FMS.

Similar to the above GT technique, Chakravarty and Shtub (1984) use the part-tool incident matrix to group parts and associated tooling simultaneously. They then use a rank order clustering algorithm to obtain part families and their associated tooling.

Mathematical Programming

The previous two approaches provide satisficing solutions to the part grouping problem. However, optimal solutions can be obtained using mathematical programming techniques. Mathematical programming has the advantage of capturing all the constraints imposed on the system.

Unlike using the similarity between parts as the basis for part grouping as used in GT techniques, Hwang (1986), and Hwang and Shogun (1989) use the constraints imposed on the system as the basis for part grouping. The constraints considered are: (1) tool magazine capacity of the system, (2) the due date of each part order, and (3) the total processing time of each tool. Hwang proposes two integer programming models. The first formulation considers the first constraint only and can be termed the optimal part grouping problem.

The second formulation considers the second constraint as well as the first constraint. Under some assumptions, Hwang shows that the second formulation reduces to the bin packing problem and knapsack problem, which are both NP-complete. The objective chosen aims to minimize the number of tool changeovers (i.e., the number of batches). Because this problem is intractable, he suggests maximizing the number of parts in a batch. Though it appears to be a good surrogate, it tends to put off the selection of the job which requires more tools. Consequently, tool commonality is not fully utilized, resulting in a larger number of part groups.

The part families problem can also be modeled as a p-median problem (Kusiak 1983). Kusiak uses the distance between two parts as a criteria to group parts. Instead of using traditional clustering algorithms for part grouping, he uses an integer programming formulation originally proposed by Rao (1971). He then proposes a subgradient algorithm to solve the problem. Hwang (1986) found that the use of integer programming for clustering analysis is inappropriate in this application.

Stecke and Kim (1987) use a flexible approach to both select part types and their production ratios to balance aggregate machine loads. They define a flexible approach as one in which decisions regarding production ratios are continuously updated whenever a part type completes its production requirements. The formulation is solely based on balancing the machine loads rather than trying to capture common processing features between part types. Kumar et al. (1986) model the part grouping problem using an optimal k-decomposition of weighted networks. Seidmann and Schweitzer (1984) use an undiscounted semi-markovian model in selecting what part type to process next. They use minimization of penalty costs as the criterion, but the cost structure is subjective.

3.3 MACHINE LOADING

The loading problem is concerned with the allocation of operations and associated tooling among a set of machines or work stations, subject to the technological and capacity constraints of the FMS. In general, the methods used in conventional job shop loading can be applied to the FMS loading problem. However, the performance is greatly diminished; because the advantages of flexibility are not used.

Complexity of FMS Loading

In a study Stecke (1983) reports that the loading problem in FMS is more difficult than in job shops. This is because: (1) the machines are more versatile and capable of performing many different operations, (2) several parts can be machined simultaneously, and (3) each part may have more than one production route. These capabilities of the FMS increase both the decision variables and the number of constraints in setting up the FMS loading problem. There are numerous studies on the FMS loading problem. A representative sample includes Stecke (1983), Berrada and Stecke (1986), Shanker and Tzen (1985), Rajagopalan (1986), Kusiak (1984), Chung (1986a, 1986b), Bernardo and Mohamed (1992), Kouvelis and Lee (1991), Sawik (1990). These formulations use different loading objectives.

Loading Objectives

Stecke (1983) proposed the following six objectives, any one of which can be used as the loading criteria:
1. Balance the assigned machine processing times.
2. Minimize the part movements or maximize the number of consecutive operations on each machine.
3. Balance the work load per machine for a system of groups of pooled machines of equal group sizes.
4. Unbalance the workload per machine for a system of groups of pooled machines of unequal sizes.
5. Fill the machine tool magazines as densely as possible.
6. Maximize the number of operation assignments.

Rationale and critical assessment of loading objectives

The objective of loading is problem dependent. For example, if it is desired to finish processing jobs around the same time, then balancing of the workload would achieve this objective. If it is desired not to move jobs between machines, then the second objective can be used. The most widely used objective in research, namely, balancing the workload, is the least practiced in industry (Smith et al. 1986). As discussed later, the six objectives can be in conflict with each other. Chung (1986a, 1986b) has critically assessed these objectives and addresses the loading problem incorporating tool efficiency.

Balancing of the workload across machines has been popular both in conventional systems and FMSs; that is, to try to make the total processing times assigned to each machine as equal as possible. The rationale is that if the workloads are uniform, there will be less congestion; and system performance will be improved. Also, this objective will make all machines finish their assigned workloads more or less at the same time, and the system can then be reconfigured to process a new batch of parts. However, Stecke (1981) points out that the practice of balancing may be too restrictive, since the flexibility of the machines may not be fully utilized.

Chakravarty and Shtub (1984) address the loading problem with an objective of minimizing the maximum sum of processing time of all machines. Although not a complete substitute, the objective of minimizing the maximum processing time can be a good surrogate for the balancing of machine loads. However, minimizing the total processing time is a greedy approach of assigning operations to those machines which have the smallest processing times. This may result in the uneven distribution of workloads among machines; consequently, it can be in conflict with the objective of balancing workloads.

The question of balancing was first raised by Buzacott and Shanthikumar (1980), and an analytical proof was provided by Shanthikumar (1982). Several extensions and simpler proofs of similar results can be found in Yao and Kim (1984). Based on empirical results, Stecke (1981) and Stecke and Morin (1985) support the optimality of balanced workloads with respect to expected production for single machine centers. However, Stecke and Solberg (1985) showed that if functionally similar machines are pooled into machine groups of equal size, then balancing maximizes expected production.

The second objective of Stecke (1983), minimizing the number of part movements, will result in unbalanced workloads with larger queue lengths near the most heavily used machines. This objective is desirable if the transportation time is significant in comparison with processing times. In some cases it is desirable to have a part remain on a machine for several consecutive operations rather than to have it moved from one machine to another for the sake of balancing

(Stecke 1983, Stecke and Solberg 1981b). If it is desirable to make use of the commonality in tooling, then minimizing the part movement is in conflict with this objective; that is, a job will stay on the same machine instead of visiting another machine to make use of the common tool. Taking advantage of the commonality in tooling requirements, parts can be grouped together for simultaneous processing (for example, refer to Chakravarty and Shtub 1984).

Using the CAN-Q model, Stecke and Solberg (1981a) conclude that the expected production is maximum if one:

1) balances the workload if all group sizes are equal, (the third loading objective of Stecke 1983).

2) unbalances the workload if group sizes are unequal (Stecke and Solberg 1985). This is the fourth loading objective of Stecke (1983).

The rationale behind the fifth and sixth loading objectives of Stecke (1981a) is to provide alternate routings. By filling tool magazines densely, several operations can be assigned to each machine, thus making the system more flexible. In this way, system performance can be enhanced through better utilization of the equipment and lower waiting times (Stecke 1983). However, the disadvantage of filling the tool magazines as densely as possible is that (1) an excessive number of tools have to be changed between two tool change-overs, and (2) those tools which require more than one slot are least preferred under this objective. But in reality, those tools may be needed as much as others. In addition, the tools should be filled after the assignment is made and not vice versa.

Different Approaches to Loading Problem

The loading problem can also be viewed as a bin packing problem. A partial list of examples include Shanker and Tzen (1985), Ammons et al. (1984), Rajagopalan (1986), Stecke and Talbot (1985). The loading problem has also been looked at as a multiple knapsack problem. Relevant papers on this topic include Morin and Marsten (1976), Hung and Fisk (1978), Harowitz and Sahni (1974), etc. These problems are NP complete.

Kusiak (1985) addresses the loading formulation from a different perspective. He formulates four loading problems based on the generalized transportation problem and the generalized assignment problem. These models differ from others in that they minimize production costs.

The first loading model takes into account the maximum allowable time of each operation on workstations. However, how to obtain this maximum allowable time is not given. The second model is an extension of the first model with an additional constraint of tool magazine capacity. The third model associates the length of tool life with the constraints of the first model. The fourth model integrates features of both the second and third models.

The formulations are integer programming (integer and boolean) and can be solved using general mixed integer techniques such as the cutting plane method or the branch and bound method. However, it may be difficult to obtain optimal solutions in a reasonable amount of time. An effective branch and bound algorithm has been suggested by Berrada and Stecke (1986). This branch and bound algorithm can solve most FMS loading problems in a reasonable length of time. Taking into account the complexity of the FMS loading problem, efficient heuristics seem inevitable. Relevant papers on this topic include Whitney and Goul (1985), and Stecke and Talbot (1985). Whitney and Goul provide a heuristic for the load balancing objective. Stecke and Talbot suggest heuristics for loading objectives: (1) minimizing part movements, (2) balancing of load if machine groups are of equal size, and (3) unbalancing of workload for machine groups of unequal size.

The loading problem has been combined with other problems. Rajagopalan (1986) formulates loading and the part type selection problem as mixed integer programming. The loading objective is to minimize the sum of total tool change-over time and processing time. Since the formulation is NP complete, he provides six heuristics. The limitations of his approach are: (1) multiple operation assignments are not allowed, (2) the completion times are assumed and independent of loading policy, and (3) the operations performed on a machine are decided only after the part is assigned to that machine.

A Categorization of Studies on Loading Problem

Smith et al. (1986) conducted a survey on 19 FMS installations in the U.S. The objective was to show the needs of the industry and how the loading/scheduling procedures developed in the research studies satisfied those needs. FMS users ranked the first three priorities as meeting due dates, maximizing system utilization, and minimizing work-in-process inventory. The loading objective of maximizing production rate scored the fourth place, minimizing set-up times took the fifth place, minimizing flow time took the sixth place, and the last place was awarded to balancing machine usage.

The results of Smith's survey bring to light the disparities in the importance attached to the loading objectives between the research studies and the users of FMS. In the existing studies, balancing of the machines and maximization of the production rate have been the popular objectives. But these objectives are not accorded with the same importance in the industry. Industry considers meeting due dates to be most important. Maximization of system utilization and minimization of the in-process-inventory are considered to be next important.

The existing studies on FMS loading is summarized in Table 3.1. The Table 3.1 lists the loading objectives and the relevant literature in the decreasing order of importance as viewed by the FMS users. The classification is based on the FMS environment which considers the length of the planning period and the type of demand. Four combinations are identified as: (1) infinite period and static demand; (2) finite period and static demand; (3) infinite period and variable demand; (4) finite period and variable demand. As indicated, most of the studies assume infinite period with static demand. But FMS is geared more towards meeting varying demands on time at low cost. Such a requirement can be met by adopting loading policies that will satisfy demand on time (due-date satisfaction) at minimum cost. To achieve this, in this study minimization of costs is chosen as the objective with finite periods. By satisfying demand in each period, due-date satisfaction is ensured. This policy will be shown to impart FMS with more flexibility implying more efficient utilization of the FMS. This study will try to incorporate three important criterion, viz., due-date satisfaction, efficient FMS utilization, and minimum inventory.

3.4 PART ROUTING

The part routing is the set of machines a part visits for processing. It is different from sequencing in that the latter has technological constraints such as precedence requirements. The part

Loading Objectives	FMS Environment			
	Infinite Period Static Demand	Finite Period Static Demand	Infinite Period Variable Dem.	Finite Period Variable Dem.
Due Date Satisfaction		Shanker & Tzen [1985]		
Maximize Sys. Utilization				
Minimize In-Process Inv.		Chakravarty & Shtub [1986]		
Maximize Production Rate	Afentakis [1986] Stecke [1986] Stecke & Solberg [1985]			
Minimize Set Up Time	Rajagopalan [1986]	Kiran & Tansel [1986]		
Minimize Flow Time	Greene &Sadowski [1986]			
Balancing Machine Usage	Stecke [1983a] Berrada & Stecke [1986] Chung [1986] Whitney & Goul [1986] Ammons et al. [1986]			

Table 3.1: Classification of Current Research on FMS Loading Problem.
Arrangement of Loading Objectives is in Decreasing Order of
Importance as Viewed by the FMS Industry.

routing has a pronounced effect on the production rate and FMS utilization. If the production mix of parts (part grouping problem) is known, and locations at which their operations are performed (loading problem) are known, then manufacturing paths need to be chosen for the parts dispatched into the system (part routing).

The common industrial practice is to route parts in such a way that the loads are balanced across workstations (Olker 1978, Solberg 1977). But the balancing of workload may not yield maximum production (Stecke and Solberg 1985). Routing paths can be found in advance, or a set of decision rules can be specified which makes real time decisions about the choice of the next workstation depending upon the status of the FMS (Buzacott 1982a). Real time control policies are useful when the machines are prone for failures (Olsder and Suri 1980, Hildebrant 1980, Kimemia and Gershwin 1983).

On-line Routing Decisions

Kimemia and Gershwin (1979) formulate the part routing problem based on alternate strategies to exploit fully the flexibility advantages of FMS. Alternate strategies could be planned to balance workloads and, in addition, can be used to respond dynamically to machine failures and temporary overloads. Their formulation is a nonlinear program, which they solve using an augmented Lagrangian method in combination with Dantzig-Wolfe decomposition. If arrival times and processing times are deterministic, the model reduces to a linear programming problem.

Kimemia and Gershwin (1983) proposed a four level hierarchical control for FMS part routing and scheduling problems. The hierarchical structure is designed to compensate for machine failures and changes in part requirements. Although the scheduling method is effective, the routing decision was not. Moreover, some of the routing decisions calculated in their method might not be feasible. In contrast with Hildebrant's work (1980), where the link between FMS and its external environment is production rate, Kimemia and Gershwin (1983) have a downstream buffer on its output side and a controller on its input side. The downstream buffer helps to decouple FMS from subsequent stages. The input controller implements decisions from the master production schedule. This input control regulates flow and determines the optimal routings. It also helps in the timely release of jobs to maintain the throughput and be in agreement with the loading decisions. Although machine breakdown is considered, the system remains in an equilibrium condition whenever failure occurs.

To include real time loading and routing decisions, Maimon and Gershwin (1988) extended the above work of Kimemia and Gershwin (1983). The FMS contains machines that fail randomly and stay down for a random length of time. They characterize the dynamic nature of the FMS by a system of nonlinear partial differential equations which do not have closed form analytical solutions. To circumvent this drawback, they propose an algorithm for loading and routing decisions. The loading decision is based on the algorithm by Gershwin et al. (1985), and Akella et al. (1984), while the routing decision is based on the algorithm by Maimon and Choong (1987).

Routing is also treated by Hahne (1981) and Tsitsiklis (1981). They maximize the system throughput in which parts are routed from an upstream machine to one of two unreliable downstream machines. They show the optimal policies to be piece-wise constant functions of intermediate buffer levels. Calculation of exact policies for the three machine system has large computational requirements. Seidman and Schweitzer (1984) consider randomness due to variations in processing times. In all cases, the full system is not considered. Instead, only one decision point is considered; and decisions are made on a purely local basis. However, Maimon and Gershwin (1988) take a global view of the system status. Both local and global decisions are made separately. Local decisions are made that are consistent with the decisions made on a global basis.

Olsder and Suri (1980) consider a system with failure prone machines. The problem is formulated as a stochastic control problem; optimality conditions are derived using dynamic programming approach. The difficulty with this approach is in obtaining closed form solutions for larger systems.

Using a queuing network model, Yao and Buzacott (1985) determine the routing of jobs which follows probabilistic shortest queue rule. According to this scheme, jobs are routed to the shortest queue with highest probability. Also, queuing network models have been used to study the effects of routing policies on the throughput and in-process inventory of an FMS (Solberg 1981, Secco Suardo 1979, Buzacott and Shanthikumar 1980, and Stecke and Solberg 1982). Suri (1981, 1983) has argued for the validity of this approach when applied to FMS.

Off-line Routing Decisions

Simulation techniques allow detailed investigation of the effects of parameter variations and routing policies (Hutchinson 1977, Shanthikumar and Sargent 1980). Simulations can be costly in terms of computation, particularly when the number of options to be tested are large. Some examples include Hutchinson and Hughes (1977), Mayer and Talvage (1976) and Draper labs (1984).

Bastos (1987) considers batching and routing problems together. With the results obtained from batching and routing, using simulation, dispatching and sequencing are performed to obtain the system output. The objective of batching and routing is to reduce the completion time of production of parts. Alternate routes exist for each part type, but the routes will be selected in the batching problem with the objective of balancing loads as evenly as possible. This requires iterating between batching and routing problems. The objective of the routing is to assign a process-plan to each part type. This assigning task attempts to minimize the time required to manufacture a batch taking into account alternate routes. Bastos concludes that efficient operation of the FMS largely depends on the results of the routing problem.

Chen (1989) used sequential decision process to solve the loading and routing problems. The results of the loading problem are used in the routing problem to select production routes that minimize the makespan. This approach has two drawbacks: (1) the selection of routes from the numerous routes (resulting from the loading problem) in the routing problem makes integer programming intractable; (2) the objectives pursued in the loading and routing problems are different. Consequently, what is the surety that the production routes resulting from the loading assignments will result in the most minimum makespan? There could be a better loading assignment set that will yield the best makespan when the routing problem is solved.

A need for solving jointly loading and routing problems

The above papers either have considered the routing problem separately or in conjunction with the loading problem. The decision process is sequential and iterative. There is no control over the number of iterations required to obtain the solution. This can be avoided by capturing both the loading problem and the routing problem in a single formulation. The solution to this joint model assigns each operation of a part type and its related tooling to a set of machines. The route(s) for a part type is/are then the set(s) of machines it visits. It is not necessary to evaluate each route of a part which would arise if the routing problem is taken separately. This reduces the problem domain and brings down the solution time. Such a joint model for the loading and routing problems will be presented in the next chapter.

3.5 SUMMARY

In this chapter, the pertinent studies on machine loading, routing, and part grouping have been discussed. Various views and approaches taken by different studies on the above subjects were explained in detail. A brief discussion is in order here to highlight the research issues.

Hierarchical planning was shown to be necessary, because FMS is a complex structure. However, there is no clear order in which these sub-problems should be solved in order to have a near optimal solution for the entire system.

Part grouping becomes necessary due to limited capacities of the tool magazines. Two prominent approaches used are the sequential approach and the group technology (GT) approach. The sequential approach results in sub-optimal grouping, whereas, the subjective nature of taking the distances between parts as a basis for part grouping in GT approach is questionable. The existing studies deals with the part grouping problem separately in spite of its effects on the other problems. This sometimes results in the infeasibility of other problems (loading problem). This drawback is overcome in this study by establishing a relationship between the loading and part grouping problems.

The priorities assigned to machine loading objectives in the research studies and industrial practice are very different. In the research studies maximizing production rate is very popular. But industry accords high importance to meeting due dates, achieving high system utilization, and minimizing inventories. In this book a loading policy is developed to reflect the needs of the industry and it is compared against the maximizing production rate objective.

In the existing studies, the routing problem has been studied separately from the loading problem. The drawback is that some of the loading decisions may result in infeasible routes when the routing problem is solved. In addition, the number of routing alternatives resulting from the loading solution may prevent exhaustive enumeration of all routes. Thus, it is critical that these two problems should be studied jointly and it is pursued in this book. Within the framework of the solutions from the joint loading and routing problem, the part grouping problem must be addressed. This hierarchy will reduce the chances of infeasible solutions.

IV

Development of Models

Chapter I introduced a generic FMS along with the planning problems faced in its operation. Current studies pertaining to the planning problems were reviewed in Chapter III which reveal the importance of establishing a hierarchical planning procedure. In a separate study O'Grady and Menon (1985) also reiterate similar concerns on the importance of hierarchical planning in complex manufacturing systems.

In this chapter, a planning hierarchy is developed to establish the relationship between the loading, routing and part grouping problems. Then, mathematical models for these problems are developed such that the formulations preserve the relationship between them.

In Section 4.1, a planning hierarchy is developed. In Section 4.2, using this hierarchy, loading and routing models are developed. In Section 4.3, a model for the part grouping problem is then developed within the guidelines provided by the loading and routing models. Finally, a summary is given in Section 4.4.

4.1 PLANNING HIERARCHY DEVELOPMENT

Stecke (1983) notes that production planning in FMS is more difficult than in assembly lines or job shops because (1) each machine is quite versatile and is capable of performing many different operations, (2) the system can process several different part types simultaneously, and (3) each part may have more than one route in the system. These additional capabilities and planning options increase both the number of decision variables and the constraints associated with FMS system set-up.

While many FMS's have been installed around the world, the capacity of these systems have been under-utilized because of the lack of proper planning procedures. Also, the efficient operation of an FMS can be very difficult, even for the most experienced shop supervisor. Any decision to allocate some resources to the production of one part necessarily affects the resources available to produce all other part types. The interaction between part types for the same resources is rather complex and not easy to predict. A good planning procedure will alleviate some of these problems.

To better utilize the inherent flexibility of an FMS, a careful system set-up (planning) is required prior to production. The five set-up problems Stecke (1983) identifies, namely; machine grouping, loading, part grouping, resource allocation, and production ratio, need to be solved before production can begin. Addressing these sub-problems in isolation can lead to an infeasible solution to the total system set-up problem. For example, when the part grouping problem is solved, it may yield a subset of parts for concurrent production whose total tool requirements may exceed the tool holding capacity of the FMS. This will result in the infeasibility in the loading problem. Although the planning sub-problems have been identified, the inter-relationship between them has not been clearly defined.

To establish the linkage between these problems, some researchers have attempted to combine all or some of these problems (see Kiran and Tansel 1986). The drawback is the computational difficulty and prohibitive time required to solve realistic FMS problems. The decision variables and the number of constraints grow exponentially with the problem size.

Further, a FMS needs to be integrated with the plant's production system. An example of this is one FMS in a Swedish company, Bygg-och Transportekonomi, which is integrated with a classical manufacturing facility as reported in Bastos (1990). Studies pertaining to FMS thus far consists of machining systems without any integration with assembly and fabrication systems (Kusiak 1986). Although a need to integrate the above systems was stressed by Kusiak, few studies have taken this approach.

The planning hierarchy proposed in this study is shown in Figure 4.1. An aggregate production plan is developed and broken down on a monthly or quarterly basis to meet the estimated production demand of the end items. This is done at the plant-wide level since FMS is just another component of this complex structure. The aggregate planning phase establishes the relationship between FMS and plant wide production planning needs. This production plan is then

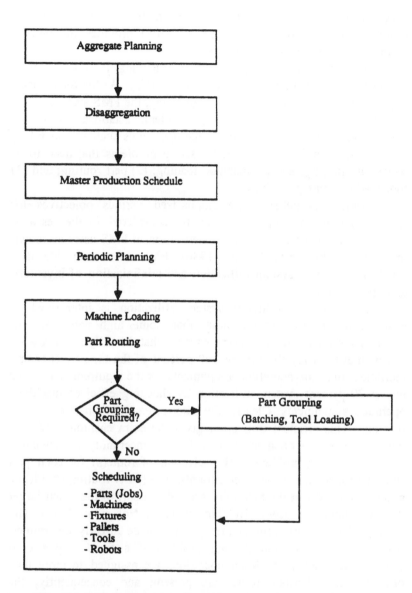

Figure 4.1: Production Planning Hierarchy.

disaggregated into time phased requirements for each part type. The resulting Master Production Schedule (MPS) provides the weekly production requirements of each part type.

Using the MPS as input, periodic planning is carried out to establish the production requirements by shift/day. Within the demand requirements established by periodic planning, the FMS system set-up problems are solved. These set-up problems establish the bridge between the aggregate plan and on-line operations such as scheduling and alternate routings. The specific set-up problems that need to be solved at this stage are: (1) machine loading; (2) part routing; and (3) tool loading (part grouping).

Various researchers have emphasized various objectives for loading. All of the objectives thus far considered in the research literature have scored poorly in the perception of FMS users as shown in a survey by Smith et al. (1986). FMS users rate due date satisfaction, higher system utilization and minimization of inventory as important objectives.

In this study, a higher system utilization is interpreted as efficient use of the system rather than some high percentage of machine/system usage. To clarify, suppose that the daily requirements can be met by using the system 100 percent of the time by choosing inefficient machine-operation assignments, or the requirements can be met at 70 percent system utilization by choosing efficient machine-operation assignments. Clearly, the latter utilization is better than the first one. This efficient utilization gives the extra cushion needed if there is a machine breakdown or if there is uncertainty in demand.

The routing problem is the selection of route(s) for each part subject to machine capacity constraints. Job (part) routing should be at the lower level of the hierarchy since it is a part of the much larger decision making process (Hutchinson 1977, Nof et al. 1979). The routing of each part through the system can be directly determined from the output of the loading problem if a fixed sequence is specified for each part. When operations are assigned to more than one machine, alternate routes are present; and consequently, the routing problem must be solved in order to determine the quantity that should be made from each route.

The part grouping (tool loading) problem is concerned with the selection of a subset of parts for concurrent production, if not all of the parts can be processed simultaneously. This may be necessary due to the tool holding capacities of the machines. The results from the loading and routing model indicate the operation assignment and quantity made from each route. At this point a check is made to determine the necessity of part grouping. If the total tools required are within the machines tool holding capacity, part grouping is not necessary.

Traditionally, GT concepts are used in part grouping and is done before loading (Stecke 1983). Suppose if the diversity in part variety does not allow part grouping, then the basis on which each part group is processed is questionable. In addition, the objective of part grouping based on GT concepts is different than the objective of the loading problem (for example makespan). Hence, the total makespan resulting from part grouping based on GT concepts may not be the optimal makespan. That is, there should be consistency in the objectives pursued. The above hierarchy allows for part grouping based on the consistency in the objectives of the loading and part grouping problems, loading assignments, and the tool magazine capacity of machines.

The scheduling problem is the dispatching of selected part types to the production routes established from the routing problem. Scheduling procedures may be on-line or off-line. On-line solutions illustrate dynamic scheduling where a decision has to be made at the end of each event. The event could be a completion of an operation, or a job, or a machine failure.

Off-line scheduling is static in nature. Since the routings are already available, the scheduling decisions can be made relatively easily. Since the machines account for about 60-75% of the investment in FMS, it is imperative not to restrict their usage by a limited number of pallets/fixtures. Depending on the number of pallets/fixture available for each part, the jobs can be sent into the system in such a way that ensures proper machine usage. The minimum number of pallets/fixtures needed to ensure proper machine usage corresponds to the number of production routes (from the loading and routing problem) used in the system. That is, the production ratio and resource allocation problems of Stecke (1983) are more suitable at this level in the hierarchy than at higher levels.

4.2 THE LOADING AND ROUTING MODEL

Assigning multiple operations to machines utilizes their versatility better besides providing alternate routes for parts. This increases the routing flexibility of an FMS. However, assigning an operation to a machine(s) depends on both the capacity available and other operations competing for the same machine(s).

For an efficient solution to a planning problem, the loading and routing problems should be studied jointly. However, all of the existing research studies have treated these two problems independently. This independent approach may result in impracticable routes (Kimemia and Gershwin 1979, 1983). Usually, the loading problem has been analyzed separately or in conjunction with the part selection problem.

The loading and routing problems have not been studied jointly. The usual approach is to solve the loading problem first, and then use its results to solve the routing problem (see Chen 1989). Though this sounds simple, it is not free of pitfalls. Suppose the loading objective is to make multiple assignments to increase the routing flexibility of the system, the resulting routing decision variables grow exponentially. To see this, suppose there are m machine and n operations to be performed. Further, let each machine be capable of performing each of all n operations. If the tool magazine capacity is not binding, then the maximum possible number of routings is equal to m^n. That is, with 5 machines and 5 operations the maximum number of routes are 3125. With 10 machines and 5 operations, the maximum number of routes would be 100,000.

But some of the routings from the loading model may not be used. Thus, the solution space of the routing model could be reduced, and this can be accomplished by studying loading and routing problems jointly. Further, it is necessary that, due to the limited capacity available in each time period, the loading and routing policies should ensure demand satisfaction. That is, if the routing problem is solved after the loading problem, there is a possibility that demand may not be satisfied in a given time period. This could be due to the selection of improper loading assignments. This means that all combinations of the loading assignments have to be exhausted before (1) it can be ascertained whether the time available to meet the demand is sufficient or not, and (2) select the optimal combination.

The demand imposed on the FMS in each period has to be satisfied. This is achieved either by producing the part types in the period required, or to inventory parts from prior periods. The aim is to try to utilize efficiently the FMS. At the same time, the policy should try to impart FMS with more system flexibility through increased routing flexibility and capacity flexibility. However, in order to increase routing flexibility, alternate routings must be allowed. This can be achieved by optimizing the loading assignments to machines subject to capacity constraints and by capturing the similarity in process features such as common tooling.

Formulation of the Constraints

Using the definitions of Table 4.1, the constraints necessary for the loading and routing problem are developed individually.

1. Machine Capacity
The machines have finite capacities (C), and production requirements have to be satisfied using these limited capacities. The workload assigned to each machine by the loading and routing model should be less than or equal to its capacity. That is,

$$\sum_{i \in I} \sum_{j \in Oi} n_{ijkt} \, P_{ijk} \leq C \qquad \forall \, k, t \tag{1}$$

2. Flow Constraint
A part may be made from several routes. However, the sum of quantities made from all routes must equal the total quantity produced in that period. A priori production routes are not selected for a part but instead let the model determine those routes. Thus, the above requirement of the sum of quantities produced from all routes equalling the total quantity produced has to be incorporated differently. This is accomplished by setting for each operation of part i, the total number of times it is performed equal to the total quantity produced of part i. The total number is obtained by summing over all machines the number of times that an operation is repeated (i.e., $n_{()}$). That is,

Table 4.1

Notation

t   {1,2,...,T} set of time periods

S   {1,2,..,i,..,s} set of part types

O_i index set of operations for part i

C   available capacity of machines in minutes

a_{it} demand of part i in period t

Q_{it} number of units of part i produced in period t

I_{it} inventory of part i in period t

n_{ijkt} number of times operation j of part i done on machine k in period t

MS_t makespan in period t

P_{ijk} processing time of operation j of part i on machine k

X_{ijkt} equals 1 if operation j of part i is assigned to machine k in period t, zero otherwise

S_m set of X_{ijkt}'s which utilize tool m

n_{ijkt} number of times the operation j of part i is performed on machine k in period t, and

P_{ijk} processing time of operation j of part i on machine k.

$$\sum_k n_{ijkt} = Q_{it} \qquad\qquad \forall\ t,\ j \in O_i,\ i \in S \qquad\qquad (2)$$

A machine may be assigned with single or multiple operations belonging to one or several part types. Thus, a machine may fall on several production routes of parts; and hence, the flexibility of the machine is utilized. A production route of a part may use one or more machines.

3. Operation Contingency

An operation can be performed once or several times only if it is assigned ($X_{()}=1$) to a machine. That is,

$$n_{ijkt} \le M\ X_{ijkt} \qquad\qquad \forall\ t,\ j \in O_i,\ i \in S \qquad\qquad (3)$$

If $X_{()}=1$, it means the operation is assigned and can be performed $n_{()}$ number of times. Even though the operation is assigned due to common tooling, it may not be performed because of insufficient machine capacity. For this constraint to work properly, M should be at least as big as the maximum of $n_{()}$. Since this is not known initially, M should be set equal to the maximum of the cumulative demand of part types.

4. Inventory Identity

The inventory identity constraint ensures that demand is satisfied in each period. The entire part quantity $Q_{()}$ can be made in the same period, or it can be inventoried from previous periods production. However, the entire quantity should satisfy the demand $a_{()}$. That is,

$$I_{it-1} + Q_{it} = a_{it} + I_{it} \qquad\qquad \forall\ t,\ i \in S \qquad\qquad (4)$$

5. Tool Commonality

If operation j of part i is assigned to machine k, then all other operations belonging to the same part or different parts that use the same tool could be assigned to machine k in order to take advantage of common tooling. That is,

$$X_{i'j'kt} - X_{ijkt} \le 0 \qquad\qquad \forall\ j' \ne j,\ j,\ i,\ X_{ijkt} \in s_m,\ k,\ t,\ m \qquad (5)$$

This equation becomes binding only when it is considered along with equations (1) and (3). To operate within C, equation (1) selects some number for $n_{i'j'kt}$ which also satisfies equation (3). This in turn must satisfy this equation.

In a study by Stecke (1983), the commonality in tooling between operations is represented by a nonlinear formulation. Each nonlinear term is linearized by introducing two additional constraints and one new integer variable. This increases the problem size and computation time. In this light, the advantage of the above formulation (constraint (5)) is clearly evident.

Objective Functions

The minimum cost objective derived in this book is a surrogate for the two most important criteria desired by the FMS users. They are (1) due date satisfaction, and (2) efficient system utilization. Due date is satisfied by admitting no backorders. Efficient utilization of the system is achieved by minimizing inventory and satisfying production demand as early as possible (with least makespan).

A least production time is obtained by minimizing the overload, which is accomplished by minimizing the maximum workload assigned to a machine. This approach tries to distribute workload equally among machines, which ensures that all machines will finish their work around the same time (Stecke and Solberg 1985).

It is assumed in this research that the operations of any part can be done in any order. Then the maximum workload assigned to a machine will also be the makespan. This study hypothesizes that the minimum cost objective is superior to the maximize production objective in terms of inventory costs, flexibility and efficient utilization of the FMS.

Minimum Cost Policy

The objective is to minimize the total inventory costs in the planning horizon along with minimizing the makespan. The inventory costs are minimized by imposing a value on the inventory carried. The objective function is,

$$\text{Minimize } \underset{t \in T}{\Sigma} \text{ MS}_t$$

Maximum Production Rate Policy

The popular objective in the existing research is to maximize production per unit time. That is, to satisfy the production requirements as early as possible. But this is same as minimizing the makespan. Hence, the objective function representation will be the same as above. The difference between these two policies lies in the way the inventory is handled. Unlike in the minimum cost policy, there is no restriction on inventory in this policy. The purpose is to satisfy the total demand of the entire planning horizon as quickly as possible even if it entails carrying inventory.

To compare the minimum cost policy with the maximum production rate policy, two formulations are required. However, both formulations are the same except that the inventory identity constraint (4), should be replaced by the following constraint for the maximum production rate policy.

$$\underset{t \in T}{\Sigma} \ Q_{it} = D_i \qquad \forall \ i \in S$$

where D_i is the total demand for part i for the entire planning horizon.

The complete loading and routing model is:
The Loading and Routing Model (Model LRM)

$$\text{Minimize } \underset{t \in T}{\Sigma} \text{ MS}_t$$

s.t.

$$\underset{i \in I \ j \in Oi}{\Sigma \ \Sigma} \ n_{ijkt} \ P_{ijk} \leq MS_t \qquad \forall \ k, t \tag{1}$$

$$\underset{k}{\Sigma} \ n_{ijkt} = Q_{it} \qquad \forall \ t, j \in O_i, i \in S \tag{2}$$

$$n_{ijkt} \leq M \ X_{ijkt} \qquad \forall \ t, j \in O_i, i \in S \tag{3}$$
$$\text{M is a large } \#$$

$$I_{it-1} + Q_{it} = a_{it} + I_{it} \qquad \forall \ t, i \in S \tag{4}$$

or

$$\underset{t \in T}{\Sigma} \ Q_{it} = D_i \qquad \forall \ i \in I \tag{4}$$

$$X_{i'j' \ kt} - X_{ijkt} \leq 0 \qquad \forall \ j' \neq j, \ j, \ i, \qquad (5)$$
$$X_{ijkt} \in s_m, \ k, \ t, \ m$$

$$MS_t \leq C \qquad \forall \ t \qquad (6)$$

$$X_{ijkt} = \{0, \ 1\} \qquad (7)$$

$$n_{ijkt}, \ I_{it}, \ Q_{it}, \ MS_t \geq 0 \ (\text{integer}) \qquad (8)$$

Discussion of tool magazine capacity

In the above LRM formulations, it is not necessary to consider explicitly tool magazine capacity, because this is handled by part grouping if required. The only capacity that is binding is the machine capacity. For example, consider an FMS that has one machine with a tool capacity of one. Assume that there are three parts to be made in a shift of eight hours, that each part requires two hours of production time, and that each part uses different tools. If a tool magazine constraint were added to LRM, the result would be to produce only one part type and back order the other two parts. However, in reality, the machine capacity of eight hours does exceed the demand capacity of six hours. The LRM result could assign all three parts to the time period. The tool constraint would require three batches of parts, each batch having one part. Consequently, to meet demand, tool capacity is not a constraint, but machine capacity is a constraint. If there exists sufficient machine capacity to produce the required number of parts but there is insufficient tool capacity as in the above example, then part grouping is required.

4.3 PART GROUPING

The results from LRM are the operation assignments to the machines, the routing decisions for each part type, and the quantities to be produced of each part type by route by period. Since the tools have to be loaded on the machine tool magazines before production begins, the operation assignments may exceed the magazine capacity. Consequently, it is necessary to group part types so that they can be produced sequentially in that planning period. This problem is called the part grouping problem.

The objective of the part grouping problem is to minimize the number of tool set-ups or minimize the number of batches (Hwang 1986). This is referred to as the optimal part grouping problem, which Hwang shows to be NP complete.

Since optimal part grouping is intractable, a surrogate objective of maximizing the number of part types in each batch can be used. This is intuitively appealing since maximizing the batch size will also maximize the utilization of the tool magazine capacities. Although this is one of the loading objectives of Stecke (1983), it was not considered to be important by Smith et al. (1986). In addition, the resulting grouping may perform poorly on makespan. There should be consistency in the objectives pursued in the part grouping and the loading and routing problems. Because due date satisfaction is important, the objective of the part grouping problem pursued in this research is to minimize the deviation in its planned makespan from the one obtained from LRM. The results of the part grouping problem yields the composition of each part group. The number of part groups needed corresponds to the maximum value of the number of tool magazine changeovers required of all machines. For each machine, a ratio of total tools assigned to its tool magazine capacity gives the number of tool magazine changeovers required. Since the ratio could yield a fraction, the result is rounded off to a next higher integer value.

Formulation of the Constraints

Before the constraints can be developed, the following notation is defined.

Decision Variables

$Z_{ig} = 1$ if part i is selected in batch g, zero otherwise.

$Y_{ckg} = 1$ if tool c needed by batch g is assigned to machine k, zero otherwise.

Input Parameters

d_{ijc} = 1 if tool c is needed by operation j of part i, zero otherwise.

K_c = # of tool slots required by tool type c.

X_{ijk} = Loading decision from Model LRM. 1 if the operation is assigned to machine k, zero otherwise.

$b_{ijck} = (X_{ijk})(d_{ijc}) = 1$ if operation j of part i needs tool type c on machine k, 0 otherwise.

$B_{ijck} = \{b_{ijck}/b_{ijck}=1, \forall j,c,k\}$: the set that gives unique correspondence between tools and part's operations.

Let

$w_{ik} = \{c/b_{ijck}=1, \forall c\}$: the set of tools required by part i on machine k.

$W_k = \Sigma_i \ w_{ik}$: the set of tools needed by all part types assigned to machine k.

1. Tool Magazine Capacity

For each machine, if the set of tools assigned, W_k, is less than the tool magazine capacity, then part grouping is not required. The set W_k depends on the operation assignment from LRM, which considers tool commonality. The total tool slots occupied by selected tool types can at most be equal to the tool magazine capacity. That is,

$$\sum_{c \in Wk} K_c \ Y_{ckg} \leq f_k \qquad \qquad \forall \ k, g \qquad \qquad (1)$$

where:

Y_{ckg} = 1 if tool c needed in batch g is assigned to machine k, 0 otherwise.

K_c = # of tool slots required by tool type c.

f_k = tool magazine capacity of machine k.

2. Contingency Constraint

A part type can be selected into a batch only if all of its related tooling, $\Sigma_k w_{ik}$, has been selected. That is,

$$b_{ijck} Z_{ig} \leq Y_{ckg} \qquad \forall\ c \in w_{ik}, k, i, g \qquad (2)$$
$$\text{and } b_{ijck} \in B_{ijck}$$

where:

$Z_{ig} = 1$ if part i is selected in batch g, 0 otherwise.

$b_{ijck} = (X_{ijk})(d_{ijc}) = 1$ if part i needs tool type c on machine k, 0 otherwise.

Objective Function

As mentioned before, the optimal part type grouping is NP complete. To overcome this difficulty, surrogate objectives are used. The method used in some of the existing studies of trying to include as many parts as possible is a good surrogate for the minimization of tool setups. But this approach does not ensure that the resulting makespan will be minimum. Since due date is very important, part grouping should try to satisfy this requirement. That is, it should try to finish processing all part types within a time close to the planned makespan, MS_t, of LRM. That is,

$$\text{Min} \sum_g AMS_g - MS_t$$

where:

AMS_g = adjusted makespan of part types in batch g.

The complete model for part grouping can be represented as:

Model PGM : for each period t

$$\text{Min} \sum_g AMS_g - MS_t$$

s.t.
$$\sum_g AMS_g - MS_t \geq 0 \qquad (1)$$

$$\sum_i \sum_{j \epsilon Oi} Z_{ig} \, n_{ijk} \, P_{ijk} \leq AMS_g \quad \forall \ k, g \tag{2}$$

$$\sum_{c \in Wk} K_c \, Y_{ckg} \leq f_k \quad \forall \ k, g \tag{3}$$

$$b_{ijck} \, Z_{ig} \leq Y_{ckg} \quad \forall \ c \in w_{ik}, \ k, i, g \tag{4}$$
$$\qquad\qquad\qquad\qquad\quad \text{and } b_{ijck} \in B_{ijck}$$

$$Y_{ckg} = \{0,1\} \quad \forall \ c, k, g \tag{5}$$

$$Z_{ig} = \{0,1\} \quad \forall \ i, g \tag{6}$$

$$AMS_g \geq 0 \quad \forall \ g \tag{7}$$

4.4 SUMMARY

Within the framework of the planning hierarchy of Section 4.1, the mathematical formulations for the loading and routing problem, and part grouping problem, were given. It was stressed that the loading and routing problems should be considered jointly. Otherwise, the routing problem becomes computationally cumbersome in evaluating all of the possible routes. The part grouping problem was defined in the light of the results from the loading and routing model. The part grouping problem occurs due to the limited tool holding capacities of the machines.

In the next chapter, hypotheses will be derived to compare the performance of an FMS planned by the minimum cost policy against the performance of an FMS that results from the maximum production rate policy.

V

Development of Hypotheses

In the previous chapter, models for the loading, routing, and part grouping problems were presented. In this chapter, eight hypotheses pertaining to the loading and routing policies and machine flexibility are derived.

Hypotheses are deduced in Section 5.1. To test these hypotheses an experimental FMS and its environment are selected in Section 5.2. The computer simulation procedure which outlines the test procedure is discussed in Section 5.3, and a summary is given in Section 5.4.

5.1 THE HYPOTHESES

The primary purpose of this study is to investigate the effects of loading objectives, tool magazine capacity, and machine flexibility on FMS characteristics such as flexibility, planned makespan, utilization, inventory, and tool loading (part grouping) problems. The results of this study are to help FMS users gain insights into how to better utilize an FMS.

Existing studies assume that management desires to achieve high FMS utilization to recover the capital invested in the FMS. Consequently, the objective chosen is to maximize the production rate even if it entails carrying inventories. On the other hand, the objective that minimizes inventory without sacrificing due date performance will result in lower inventory compared to maximum production rate policy. The worst performance may parallel that of the maximum production rate policy. Because of the way minimum cost policy was developed in the previous chapter, it can be said that the minimum cost policy results in significantly lower inventory than the maximum production rate policy.

The minimum cost policy gives preference to a production plan that exactly meets demand in each time period. Hence, numerous production routes would be required to meet the demand for all of the parts. The maximum production rate policy would attempt to produce the items in as short a production time as possible. Consequently, for each time period, fewer production routes would be planned; but each route should be utilized more. The following hypothesis results:

Hypothesis 1

> *A minimum cost policy imparts relatively greater routing flexibility to an FMS than a maximum production rate policy.*

The maximum production rate policy strives to satisfy total demand as early as possible within the planning horizon. Consequently, production time is minimized resulting in a lower planned makespan compared to the minimum cost policy. The term planned makespan is used because the actual makespan is not known until after scheduling. This yields the following hypothesis:

Hypothesis 2

> *A maximum production rate policy yields a production plan that has a lower planned makespan than does a minimum cost policy.*

Because the maximum production rate objective gives preference to satisfying part demand as quickly as possible, it should be expected that more production time remains to react to external disturbances in the form of changing demand. Since this is measured by capacity flexibility, the following hypothesis results:

Hypothesis 3

> *A maximum production rate policy imparts greater capacity flexibility to an FMS than a minimum cost policy.*

The minimum cost policy gives preference to a production plan that exactly meets demand in each period. Hence, more routes are used in the production of parts than if a maximum production rate policy were followed. This requires more tool slots and consequently results in more part groupings than a maximum production rate policy. This yields the following hypothesis:

Hypothesis 4

A maximum production rate policy results in fewer part groups than a minimum cost policy.

Machine flexibility is a strategic issue and relates to FMS hardware. Naturally, an FMS with a higher machine flexibility is expected to perform better than one with a lower machine flexibility. For the same production requirements, an FMS with a lower machine flexibility will require more production time to satisfy demand than an FMS with a higher machine flexibility. Consequently, the following hypothesis results:

Hypothesis 5

An FMS with a lower machine flexibility results in a relatively higher planned makespan compared to an FMS with a higher machine flexibility.

Since an FMS with a lower machine flexibility is hypothesized to result in higher production times, less production time is available for reacting to external disturbances in the form of changing demand. Since this is measured by capacity flexibility, the following hypothesis results:

Hypothesis 6

An FMS with a lower machine flexibility results in relatively lower capacity flexibility than an FMS with a higher machine flexibility.

Lower machine flexibility implies restrictions on machine-operation feasibilities. When such an FMS is used to satisfy production requirements of parts, fewer production routes are used because of the machine flexibility limitation. Consequently, it will have lower routing flexibility than an FMS with higher machine flexibility. This yields the following hypothesis:

Hypothesis 7

An FMS with a lower machine flexibility has relatively lower routing flexibility than does an FMS with a higher machine flexibility.

From the preceding discussions it can be interpreted that higher machine flexibility should improve the performance of FMS. Such an FMS should have higher routing flexibility, capacity flexibility, and a lower planned makespan. Since under maximum production rate policy inventory is not restricted and also that lower machine flexibility restricts capacity, it is expected that an FMS with a higher machine flexibility will carry higher inventory. The following hypothesis results:

Hypothesis 8

An FMS with a higher machine flexibility results in relatively higher inventory than does an FMS with a machine flexibility.

5.2 THE EXPERIMENT DESIGN

This section deals with the design of the experimental method to test the above hypotheses and to study the relationships between demand variability, loading and routing objectives, the machine flexibility, tool magazine capacity limitation, and FMS system characteristics.

In a study Jaikumar (1986) reports that the average FMS utilization in the U.S. is 52%. However, the study by Smith et al. (1986) reports the same to vary from 30% to 90%, but most of the values fall in between 60% to 75%. To keep this study close to reality, these utilization levels are considered at the data selection stage. This requirement will ensure the feasibility of solutions, and help facilitate the study of the relationship between flexibility and machine utilization, which has not been addressed in the existing studies.

Existing studies also fail to give insights into the effects of FMS hardware constraints. In this study machine flexibility and tool magazine capacity limitation are considered as FMS hardware constraints. Two levels of machine flexibility are considered. A 100% machine flexibility assumes that all of the machines could perform all of the operations for all of the parts. A 75% machine flexibility was assumed by allowing only 75% commonality between operations and machines. Two levels of tool magazine capacity are considered. First, a capacity of five tool slots is considered. Second, a continuous tool delivery system which virtually makes tool magazine capacity limitless is chosen. The latter is the current development in FMS.

The complete research design is tabulated in Table 5.1. The following sections deal with the specifics of experimental design.

The FMS and the Data Sets

The FMS configuration and data sets are developed using available information on FMS. The raw results of this study are given in Appendix A.

In order to study the effects of machine flexibility, tool magazine capacity, operating policies, and changes in part type demand the experiment data is selected based on available information reported in the existing studies. Specifically, it will be based on the findings reported by Ito (1987), Shanker and Tzen (1985), Mortimer (1984), Smith et al. (1986), Edghill and Creswell (1985), and Kochan (1985).

Mortimer (1984) and Kochan (1985) found in their surveys that a medium size FMS consists of four to six machines. In this study, five machines are included. Since more than 80% of the machines contained in FMSs are machining centers, all five machines are considered to be machining centers, but with varying efficiency. That is, no one machine is superior over other machines in terms of the processing times needed for the operations of all parts.

Table 5.1: Experiment Design.

Parameters	Treatment	Number of Treatments
Production Demand	Uniform (10-30) units	1
Part Type Distribution	1) Uniform (4-8) 2) Right Triangular (4-8) 3) Left Triangular (4-8) 4) Symmetric Unimodal (4-8)	4
Machine Flexibility	1) 100% Machine Flexibility 2) 75% Machine Flexibility	2
Tool Magazine Capacity	1) 5 Tool Slots 2) Continuous Tool Delivery	2
Loading & Routing Objectives	1) Minimum Cost Policy 2) Maximize Production Rate Policy	2
Total Number of Cases = 32		

In this study, the planning horizon is composed of time periods. The length of a time period is arbitrary as is the number of time periods in the planning horizon. However, acknowledging the enormous amount of computational time involved in solving integer programming problems (formulated in Chapter III) and to keep the problems tractable, each planning horizon is considered to be made of three time periods and each time period to be comprised of three shifts.

Sarin and Chen (1987) note that in any given planning period, the number of part types is usually very limited. Three to six part types are considered in O'Grady and Menon (1987). In this study, the number of part types for each time period is randomly chosen between four and eight from four distributions: uniform, symmetric unimodal, left triangular, and right triangular in separate studies. The quantity demanded for each part type was randomly chosen from a uniform distribution that ranged from 10 to 30 units for each part. This is to simulate the changing part type demands and varying production requirements imposed on the FMS.

Sarin and Chen (1987) found that since similar operations can be grouped to form one large operation, the number of operations can be considerably reduced. Sarin and Chen, and Lashkari et al. (1987) estimate the average number of operations to be around four. In the analysis pursued, each part type is chosen to require one to five operations, with corresponding operation times ranging from 6 to 30 minutes randomly chosen from a uniform distribution. Once the operation times are chosen they are kept the same throughout the study. In the case of 75% machine flexibility, 25% machine - operation assignments were considered infeasible.

There is a total of 24 operations. Six of them share two different tools; a total of twenty tool types are required. In a study of an FMS in Scotland, O'Grady and Menon (1987) also found 20 types of tools being used. Sarin and Chen (1987) also consider a similar number of tools. Two sizes of tool magazine capacities are considered. In the first case each machine is considered to have a limited tool magazine capacity to hold five tools to make the study conducive to part grouping. In the second case it was assumed that each machine can accommodate all twenty tools, or tool transportation is available. This situation is referred to as unlimited tool magazine capacity in this study. In the simulations, machines are kept the same for both levels of tool magazine capacities.

The data sets chosen impose variable requirements on the FMS over the planning horizon. Hence, the results will be robust in that they were obtained from analyzing many replications of the short run requirements of the FMS.

The published FMS research literature has not dealt with the number of replications needed to establish results. Shanker and Tzen (1985) used 10 replications. Due to the time consuming nature of large scale pure integer programming, 10 replications are also used in this research. The loading and routing model LRM has 568 constraints and 811 integer variables with 360 variables as 0 - 1 integer variables. After solving the loading and routing model, the part grouping model PGM is solved if needed. The need does not arise in continuous tool delivery systems but may arise in the case of limited tool magazine capacity. In the simulations pursued, the analysis of LRM output resulted in only two part groups when it was required. Based on two part groupings, the PGM model which is also a pure integer program, has 221 constraints and 218 integer variables. The total number of integer programs solved can range from a minimum of 160 (2 levels of machine flexibility X 2 loading objectives X 4 distributions X 10 replications) to a maximum of 1120 ((2 X 2 X 4 X 10 X 3 periods X 2) part groups + 160 loading & routing problems). In this research, the total number of integer programs solved was 964. These problems were solved using the MIP program of IBM on IBM 3090 super computer. SAS analysis package was used in the statistical analyses, and a significance level of .05 was used to test hypotheses.

The Performance Measures

In Chapter II, measures for three types of flexibility were developed. The measures were expressed with respect to a part type. To determine the overall flexibility of the system for each flexibility measure, the above quantities must be summed over all part types. The sum was weighted with respect to the percent of total quantity demanded in each period. The aggregate measures given in Figure 2.1 are repeated here in Figure 5.1.

$$ARF_{it} = 1 - \frac{1}{PR_{it}}$$

$$PRF_{it} = 1 - \frac{1}{AR_{it}}$$

$$CF_{it} = \frac{extra\ units\ of\ part\ i\ that\ can\ be\ made\ from\ all\ routes}{Average\ Demand\ of\ part\ i}$$

$$FMS\ ARF = \sum_t \frac{\sum_i D_{it}}{\sum_t \sum_i D_{it}} \sum_i ARF_{it} \frac{D_{it}}{\sum_i D_{it}}$$

$$FMS\ PRF = \sum_t \frac{\sum_i D_{it}}{\sum_t \sum_i D_{it}} \sum_i PRF_{it} \frac{D_{it}}{\sum_i D_{it}}$$

$$FMS\ CF = \sum_t \frac{\sum_i D_{it}}{\sum_t \sum_i D_{it}} \sum_i CF_{it} \frac{D_{it}}{\sum_i D_{it}}$$

where :

PR_i = *Production Routes for part i in period t*

AR_i = *Available Routes for part i in period t*

ARF = *Actual Routing Flexibility*

PRF = *Potential Routing Flexibility*

CF = *Capacity Flexibility*

Figure 5.1: Aggregate Flexibility Measures.

Recall that the aggregate flexibility measures represent the average ability of the system to handle internal and external disturbances given the production plan. These measures are sensitivity measures in that they represent the bounds on the disturbances beyond which the system would not be able to respond. For example, a FMS CF = 0.3 means that after satisfying the average demand imposed, the FMS still has enough capacity to meet an extra 30% of the average demand.

This extra demand may come from a surge in production requirements or machine failures. In the case of machine failures, the above implication means that the FMS can satisfy the given production requirements only if the capacity lost due to failures is less than or equal to the FMS CF. In this sense, the higher the bounds, or flexibility measures, the larger the disturbance the system can handle.

Besides flexibility measures, other important system characteristics are utilization, makespan, and inventory measured as part periods. Due date performance and efficient system utilization are two most critical FMS performance criteria (Smith et al. 1986, Stecke et al. 1989). Due date performance is satisfied by reducing makespan and avoiding backlogging. Since backlogs are not allowed, due date satisfaction is guaranteed. The difference between utilizing FMS efficiently or not depends on the inventory carried to satisfy the due date performance. A system which satisfies due date performance with lower inventory is regarded as a more efficient system.

The FMS utilization is,

$$FMS\ \mu = \frac{1}{3} \sum_{t=1}^{3} \frac{1}{5} \sum_{k=1}^{5} \frac{MS_t - S_{tk}}{1440}$$

where:
MS_t = Makespan in period t,
S_{tk} = Slack in machine k in period t, and
FMS μ = FMS utilization.

5.3 THE SIMULATION PROCEDURE

The implementation of the solution procedure is adopted from the planning hierarchy developed earlier. Extensive computer programs were developed to automate the solution procedure. Integration of all these programs with an interface will help the FMS manager make on-line decisions. A computer program was written to take the part type and their demand requirements into consideration and write an output file of model LRM in MPSX format for use in MIP solution procedure. The following computer simulation procedure, which is represented in Figure 5.2, was adopted:

Step 1. Generate all the data sets.

Step 2. Formulate the LRM model for each data set using the computer program.

Step 3. Execute the MIP procedure on the LRM formulation.

Step 4. Analyze the results from LRM model to see if part grouping is required. Appendix B contains a computer program to accomplish this task.

Step 5. Calculate the capacity flexibility and inventory at this point. Model formulation that calculates capacity flexibility is given in Appendix C.

Step 6. Determine the necessity for part grouping in the case of limited tool magazine. If grouping is needed, use model PGM and MIP solution procedure to determine the parts for simultaneous processing.

Step 7. Calculate the actual routing flexibility and potential routing flexibility for the part types chosen in a batch. A computer program and its typical output is given in Appendix D.

Step 8. Compile all the results on FMS system characteristics for each case for later use in statistical analysis for hypotheses testing.

5.4 SUMMARY

Hypotheses were developed to test the significance and the amount of changes the operating policies, and FMS hardware restrictions, have on FMS characteristics. To aid in the analysis and for hypotheses testing, an experimental FMS and its environment were designed to emulate a FMS and conditions found in practice. Performance measures used in evaluations are then provided. To operationalize the testing procedure, computer simulation procedures were presented in Section 5.3. The next chapter presents the results and discusses the statistical analyses and other important research findings.

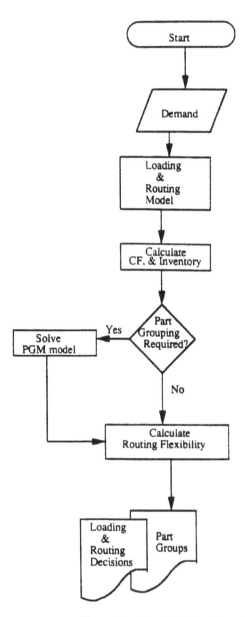

Figure 5.2: The Simulation Procedure.

VI

Results and Discussions

The previous chapter dealt with the development of hypotheses, experimental design, data, and the simulation procedure which is a blueprint of how the analyses is conducted. This chapter deals with the testing of hypotheses and discusses the insights gained from the analyses.

In Section 6.1, a detailed analysis of the results of hypotheses testing under uniform distribution is given. Sections individually discussing the results of the other three distributions, namely; symmetric unimodal, left triangular, and right triangular are not given since a comprehensive analysis for all distributions is provided in Section 6.2. Further, it avoids duplication and preserves the clarity of the results and brings forth the effects loading policies and other factors on FMS characteristics more effectively. In Section 6.3, conclusions on hypotheses testing are given.

6.1 HYPOTHESES TESTING UNDER UNIFORM DISTRIBUTION

The hypotheses developed in the previous chapter can be divided into two categories: hypotheses related to loading policies, and hypotheses related to FMS hardware constraints. The test results are discussed in the same order to bring forth the effects of loading policies and hardware limitations on FMS characteristics more vividly.

Hypotheses Related to Loading Policies

A uniform distribution over four to eight part types was used in generating the number of part types for each period, and their demand

81

(quantity) requirements were then generated using a uniform distribution over 10 to 30 units. For each simulated demand pattern, the results of the LRM minimum cost and maximum production rate formulations were obtained. The three measures of operational flexibility and inventory represented as part periods were then calculated along with the planned makespan for each LRM objective. Since the simulated demand patterns and the FMS were the same for each of the two LRM objectives, paired difference tests were performed. Tables 6.1 through 6.4 summarize the results of 10 simulation runs for each of the FMS machine flexibility and tool magazine capacity assumptions.

Before discussing the results for the flexibility measures and the planned makespan, it should be noted that the inventory results are what is to be expected. The minimum cost objective reduced average inventory, measured as part-periods, by 42.2% for the 100% machine flexibility scenario and by 35.02% in the 75% machine flexibility case. Both measures were significant at the .0001 and .0008 levels, respectively. The percent measure for the inventory indicates the proportion of average total units held in inventory. The average total units demanded during the planning horizon is calculated over 10 simulation runs.

The inventory results are what is to be expected. The maximum production rate policy strives to satisfy production requirements as early as possible. Consequently, it does not penalize the resulting inventory; whereas the minimum cost policy tries to satisfy demand keeping inventory as low as possible.

Hypothesis 1

> *A minimum cost policy imparts relatively greater routing flexibility to an FMS than a maximum production rate policy.*

This hypothesis is discussed with respect to both actual routing flexibility (ARF) and potential routing flexibility (PRF). ARF is computed using the actual routes used in the production. PRF is computed using all available routes which includes both actual production routes and potential routes created by filling left over tool

Table 6.1: Paired difference test results for 100% machine flexible FMS with limited tool magazine capacity under uniform distribution.[1,2]

System Characteristics	Difference Average	Percent[4]	Significance Level
ARF	.055	9.95	.0019
PRF	.032	3.89	.0498
CF	-.01	-.90	not significant
Adjusted Planned[3] Makespan	-21.8	-.73	not significant
Inventory Part-Periods	-162.4	-42.2	.0001

[1]All differences are calculated as the minimum cost policy result minus the maximum production rate policy result.

[2]A positive entry for ARF, PRF, and CF and negative entry for Makespan, and Inventory favors minimum cost policy.

[3]If required, part grouping was accomplished to insure feasibility of the production plan.

[4]The percent is calculated with respect to the average value of that characteristic under maximum production rate policy.

Table 6.2: Paired difference test results for 100% machine flexible FMS with continuous tool delivery system under uniform distribution.[1,2]

System Characteristics	Difference Average	Percent[3]	Significance Level
ARF	.103	16.66	.0002
PRF	0	0	not significant
CF	-.01	-.90	not significant
Planned Makespan	26.9	1.01	.003
Inventory Part-Periods	-162.4	-42.2	.0001

[1]All differences are calculated as the minimum cost policy result minus the maximum production rate policy result.

[2]A positive entry for ARF, PRF, and CF and negative entry for Makespan, and Inventory favors minimum cost policy.

[3]The percent is calculated with respect to average value of that characteristic under maximum production rate policy.

Table 6.3: Paired difference test results for 75% machine flexible FMS with limited tool magazine capacity under uniform distribution.[1,2]

System Characteristics	Difference		Significance Level
	Average	Percent[4]	
ARF	.039	6.83	not significant
PRF	.038	4.63	not significant
CF	.019	2.53	not significant
Adjusted Planned[3] Makespan	-39.5	-1.15	not significant
Inventory Part-Periods	-134.9	-35.02	.0008

[1]All differences are calculated as the minimum cost policy result minus the maximum production rate policy result.

[2]A positive entry for ARF, PRF, and CF and negative entry for Makespan, and Inventory favors minimum cost policy.

[3]If required, part grouping was accomplished to insure feasibility of the production plan.

[4]The percent is calculated with respect to the average value of that characteristic under maximum production rate policy.

Table 6.4: Paired difference test results for 75% machine flexible FMS with continuous tool delivery system under uniform distribution.[1,2]

System Characteristics	Difference		Significance Level
	Average	Percent[3]	
ARF	.053	8.6	not significant
PRF	0	0	not significant
CF	.019	2.53	not significant
Planned Makespan	20.0	.65	not significant
Inventory Part-Periods	-134.9	-35.02	.0008

[1]All differences are calculated as the minimum cost policy result minus the maximum production rate policy result.

[2]A positive entry for ARF, PRF, and CF and negative entry for Makespan, and Inventory favors minimum cost policy.

[3]The percent is calculated with respect to average value of that characteristic under maximum production rate policy.

slots. Since the tool magazine capacity is a limitation, the hypotheses have to be further analyzed considering this limitation.

The above hypothesis was strongly confirmed for ARF by the experiments for 100% machine flexibility under both limited tool magazine capacity and unlimited tool magazine capacity (continuous tool delivery system). As shown in Table 6.1, the minimum cost policy increased ARF by 9.95% in the case of limited tool magazine capacity. In the case of continuous tool delivery system, as shown in Table 6.2, this policy increased ARF by 16.66%. This is to be expected since maximum production rate policy strives to satisfy demand as early as possible using fewer production routes. This increase in actual routing flexibility was significant at .0019 and .0002 levels under limited and unlimited tool magazine capacities, respectively.

This hypothesis was not supported for actual routing flexibility for 75% machine flexibility FMS. However, with minimum cost policy ARF increased by 6.83% as shown in Table 6.3, and by 8.6% as shown in Table 6.4, under limited and unlimited tool magazine capacity respectively. That is, as the flexibility of the machines to perform operations decrease, the difference between loading and routing policies decrease. This result should be expected. In the extreme, a transfer line has no alternate tool loading or part routing decisions to be made. The closer an FMS is to a transfer line, that is, the lower the percent of operations that can be performed on all machines, the lower the number of choices for tool loading and part routing decisions. The implication of this result is that as the machine flexibility of the FMS decreases, there will not be a statistically significant difference between the two loading and routing objectives.

Hypothesis one for potential routing flexibility (PRF) was supported for 100% machine flexibility FMS under limited tool magazine capacity as shown in Table 6.1. This is statistically significant at .0498 level and resulted in an increase in PRF by 3.89%. However, it was not statistically significant for the unlimited tool magazine capacity case as shown in Table 6.2. This is to be expected. Since there is no limitation on the tool magazine capacity, all types of tools can be assigned to each machine. Thus, irrespective of the loading and routing objective, there is a limiting value for potential routing flexibility.

However, hypothesis one for potential routing flexibility was not statistically significant for 75% machine flexible FMS under both limited and unlimited tool magazine capacities as shown in Tables 6.3 and 6.4. In the case of limited tool magazine capacity, both policies do not impart much freedom due to the limitation on operation-machine feasibilities. Despite this drawback, as shown in Table 6.3, the minimum cost policy still results in an improvement of PRF by 4.63%. In the case of unlimited tool magazine capacity, the reasons given above for 100% machine flexibility hold. Thus, there is no significant difference between the two loading and routing objectives in the PRF characteristic.

Hypothesis 2

> *A maximum production rate policy yields a production plan that has a lower planned makespan than does a minimum cost policy.*

This hypothesis was confirmed only for a 100% machine flexible FMS with unlimited tool magazine capacity. As shown in Table 6.2, the result was statistically significant at .003 level with an increase of 26.9 minutes, that is 1.01%, in planned makespan under minimum cost policy. However, this hypothesis was not confirmed for limited tool magazine case as shown in Table 6.1. Because of the limitation on the number of tools that can be loaded on FMS, the policies necessitate grouping of parts. Thus, the resulting makespan from part grouping is the adjusted makespan. This adjusted makespan was not statistically significant, but the results are in favor of minimum cost policy. An average of 21.8 minutes can be conserved resulting in a saving of 0.73%.

Hypothesis two was not confirmed for 75% machine flexible FMS under both limited and unlimited tool magazine capacities. This is to be expected. When the choices are reduced, both policies do not have much freedom and will result in identical policies as they converge to the absolute case of limitation, that is, a transfer line. In the case of limited tool magazine capacity, as shown in Table 6.3, the minimum cost policy outperforms maximum production rate policy by conserving on the average 39.5 minutes, which translates to a saving of 1.15% in adjusted planned makespan. However, when the tool magazine is unlimited, the planned makespan increases by 20 minutes, that is, by .65% under minimum cost policy as shown in Table 6.4.

Most FMS's have limitations on tool magazine capacity. Besides imparting higher routing flexibilities, the minimum cost policy also results in shorter adjusted planned makespans compared to the maximum production rate policy. Since the existing research has emphasized the maximum production rate policy, the advantage of using minimum cost policy cannot be neglected. However, as the differences in adjusted planned makespans are not statistically significant, this implies that maximum production rate policy does not yield a shorter planned makespan than the minimum cost policy.

Hypothesis 3

A maximum production rate policy imparts greater capacity flexibility to an FMS than does a minimum cost policy.

This hypothesis was not supported under both machine flexibility levels. The differences are not statistically significant as shown in Tables 6.1 and 6.3. Hence, it can be concluded that statistically a maximum production rate policy does not out-perform a minimum cost policy with respect to capacity flexibility.

Although the differences are not significant, the analysis from Table 6.1 shows that in the case of 100% machine flexibility, the minimum cost policy reduces capacity flexibility by 0.9%. But in the case of 75% machine flexibility, it increases capacity flexibility by 2.53% as shown in Table 6.3. In practice, FMS's are not 100% machine flexible and do have limitation on the size of the tool magazine. The benefits of minimum cost policy are obvious. That is, the minimum cost policy imparts some savings in the planned makespan and at the same time increases capacity flexibility.

Hypothesis 4

A maximum production rate policy results in fewer part groups than a minimum cost policy.

A production plan that uses more production routes is construed to have more part groups when the tool magazine capacity is a limitation. In the case of continuous tool delivery system (unlimited tool magazine capacity), the result is trivial. That is, all parts required for production are grouped into one batch. The difference in performance becomes obvious only when the tool magazine capacity is a limitation. However, as shown in Table 6.5, the difference in the number of part groups was not statistically significant.

The minimum cost policy results in 0.4 more groups in the case of 100% machine flexible FMS and 0.6 more groups in the case of 75% machine flexible FMS. Since the differences are not statistically significant, this hypothesis can be rejected. Even though the minimum cost policy did result in more part groups, it does not increase the adjusted planned makespan. In fact, the adjusted planned makespan is shorter with a minimum cost policy. This implies that the maximum production policy does not yield fewer part groups than does the minimum cost policy.

Hypotheses Related to Machine Flexibility

The following results, as shown in Tables 6.6 through 6.9, pertain to the effect of machine flexibility on system characteristics. For each demand pattern and for each loading objective, LRM results were obtained for 100% machine flexibility and 75% machine flexibility. The inventory measures, ARF, PRF, CF, and the planned makespan, were then calculated for each machine flexibility level. Since the simulated demand patterns, loading objectives, and tool magazine capacities were the same, paired difference tests were performed.

Hypothesis 5

An FMS with a lower machine flexibility results in a relatively higher planned makespan compared to an FMS with a higher machine flexibility.

Table 6.5: Paired difference test on number of part groups.

Distri-bution	100% Machine Flexibility		75% Machine Flexibility	
	Difference Avg. %	Level	Difference Avg. %	Level
Uniform	.4 7.8	NS	.6 13.3	NS
Left Triangular	.9 20	.02	.4 8	NS
Right Triangular	.5 10.2	NS	.6 12.2	NS
Symmetric Unimodal	1.2 27.9	.003	1.0 23.8	.015

NS = Not significant

Table 6.6: Machine flexibility paired difference test results for FMS with limited tool magazine capacity under uniform distribution with the maximum production rate policy.[1,2]

System Characteristics	Difference Average	Percent[3]	Significance Level
ARF	.013	2.4	not significant
PRF	.008	.95	not significant
CF	-.383	-34.44	.0001
Planned Makespan	463	15.51	.0012
Inventory Part-Periods	-23.9	-14.75	not significant

[1]A positive entry means an increase in that characteristic for 75% machine flexibility.

[2]A negative entry means a decrease in that characteristic for 75% machine flexibility.

[3]The percent is calculated with respect to the average value of that characteristic under 100% machine flexibility.

Table 6.7: Machine flexibility paired difference test results for FMS with continuous tool delivery system under uniform distribution with the maximum production rate policy. [1,2]

System Characteristics	Difference Average	Percent[3]	Significance Level
ARF	0	0	not significant
PRF	-.014	-1.4	.0001
CF	-.383	-34.44	.0001
Planned Makespan	433	16.31	.0001
Inventory Part-Periods	-23.9	-14.75	not significant

[1]A positive entry means an increase in that characteristic for 75% machine flexibility.

[2]A negative entry means a decrease in that characteristic for 75% machine flexibility.

[3]The percent is calculated with respect to the average value of that characteristic under 100% machine flexibility.

Table 6.8: Machine flexibility paired difference test results for FMS with limited tool magazine capacity under uniform distribution with the minimum policy.[1,2]

System Characteristics	Difference		Significance Level
	Average	Percent[3]	
ARF	-.003	-.55	not significant
PRF	.014	1.66	not significant
CF	-.354	-32.12	.0001
Planned Makespan	445.4	15.03	.0001

[1]A positive entry means an increase in that characteristic for 75% machine flexibility.

[2]A negative entry means a decrease in that characteristic for 75% machine flexibility.

[3]The percent is calculated with respect to the average value of that characteristic under 100% machine flexible FMS.

Table 6.9: Machine flexibility paired difference test results for FMS with continuous tool delivery system under uniform distribution with the minimum policy. [1,2]

System Characteristics	Difference		Significance Level
	Average	Percent[3]	
ARF	-.051	-7.08	.0123
PRF	-.013	-1.37	.0001
CF	-.354	-32.12	.0001
Planned Makespan	424.3	15.82	.0001

[1]A positive entry means an increase in that characteristic for 75% machine flexibility.

[2]A negative entry means a decrease in that characteristic for 75% machine flexibility.

[3]The percent is calculated with respect to the average value of that characteristic under 100% machine flexible FMS.

This hypothesis was confirmed for FMS's with both limited and unlimited tool magazine capacities, under both loading and routing objectives. The differences are statistically significant.

Under the maximum production rate policy, the planned makespan increases for 75% machine flexible FMS by 463 minutes (15.5%) under limited tool magazine capacity as shown in Table 6.6, and by 433 minutes (16.3%) under unlimited tool magazine capacity case as shown in Table 6.7. Both differences are significant at statistical levels of .0012 and .0001, respectively.

A similar effect is seen under minimum cost policy, too. The planned makespan increases for 75% machine flexible FMS by 445 minutes (15%) under limited tool magazine capacity as shown in Table 6.8, and by 424 minutes (15.8%) under unlimited tool magazine capacity case as shown in Table 6.9. Both are significant at the statistical level of .0001.

This result is to be expected. As the machine flexibility is constrained, the available choices reduce. Consequently, the planned makespan increases.

Hypothesis 6

An FMS with a lower machine flexibility results in a relatively lower capacity flexibility compared to an FMS with a higher machine flexibility.

This hypothesis was confirmed under both objectives at the .0001 level. The capacity flexibility for a 75% machine flexible FMS decreases by 34.44% under the maximum production rate policy as shown in Table 6.6 and by 32.12% under minimum cost policy as shown in Table 6.8. This is to be expected. Because of the restriction on feasibility of some operation-machine assignments, to satisfy the same demand requirements, a 75% machine flexible FMS takes more planned makespan. Consequently, less production time is left over after satisfying the production requirements. But capacity flexibility is a measure of this slack in production time; and hence, 75% machine flexible FMS has lower CF compared to 100% machine flexible FMS.

Hypothesis 7

An FMS with a lower machine flexibility results in a relatively lower routing flexibility compared to an FMS with a higher machine flexibility.

This hypothesis was not confirmed for ARF and PRF under both loading and routing policies for an FMS with limited tool magazine capacity. The differences were not statistically significant as shown in Tables 6.6 and 6.8. When the results were compared under unlimited tool magazine capacity, no significant difference was found for ARF under maximum production rate objective as shown in Table 6.7. This result is to be expected. The maximum production rate objective makes no effort to utilize multiple routes. Under minimum cost policy, the difference was significant at the .0123 level for ARF as shown in Table 6.9. However, under both policies, for PRF, the differences were significant at the .0001 level as shown in Tables 6.7 and 6.9.

The above results imply that if there is a limited tool magazine capacity, lower machine flexibility can be partly compensated for by an increased routing flexibility. It should be emphasized that the minimum cost objective not only imparts greater flexibility to an FMS for a given machine flexibility, but it also allows for larger improvements in flexibility as the machine flexibility increases.

Hypothesis 8

An FMS with a higher machine flexibility results in a relatively higher inventory compared to an FMS with a lower machine flexibility.

This hypothesis was not confirmed. Even though the difference is not statistically significant as shown in Table 6.6, a 75% machine flexible FMS carries 14.75% lower inventory compared to a 100% machine flexible FMS. This is because 100% machine flexibility imparts no restriction to an FMS operating under maximum production rate policy. Consequently, this FMS has more capacity than an FMS with 75% machine flexibility. Since the maximum production rate policy strives to satisfy production requirements as early as possible, it results in higher inventory. Since 100% machine flexible FMS has more capacity compared to 75% machine flexible FMS, it is expected to carry higher inventory.

6.2 SUMMARY OF THE RESULTS OF ALL FOUR DISTRIBUTIONS

Comparison of Policies

Table 6.10 represents the relative percent improvement and statistical level for the FMS operating characteristics when the minimum cost policy is applied instead of the maximum production rate policy. The following paragraphs discuss the results with respect to Table 6.10.

When the tool magazine is limited, a significant improvement is seen for actual routing flexibility, ARF, under both machine flexibility levels. However, as the machine flexibility level decreases, relative improvement also decreases. This means the minimum cost policy not only imparts greater flexibility to an FMS for a given machine flexibility, but it allows for larger improvements in flexibility as the machine flexibility increases. This benefit is obtained by sacrificing adjusted planned makespan marginally. Though there is an increase in the makespan, it is not significant. A comparatively higher improvement is seen in the potential routing flexibility in the case of 75% machine flexibility. This means the minimum cost policy creates more alternate routes than the maximum production rate policy as the machine flexibility reduces. That is, the minimum cost policy yields maximum routing flexibility.

When the FMS is equipped with a continuous tool delivery system, the maximum potential routing flexibility attained is the same under both policies. This is due to no limitations on the maximum operations that can be assigned to a machine. However, the actual routing flexibility shows significant improvement with the minimum cost policy, relatively higher in the case of 100% machine flexibility.

Table 6.10: Summary of results on all distributions.

System Measure	100% machine flexibility, limited tool magazine capacity							
	Percentage				Significance level			
	UNIF	LTD	RTD	SUD	UNIF	LTD	RTD	SUD
ARF	9.95	17.2	14.2	11.8	.002	.033	.024	NS
PRF	3.89	4.92	2.0	1.5	.05	.032	NS	
CF	-0.9	6.76	-2.0	3.6	NS			
APMS	-.73	1.82	.75	1.2	NS			
INV	-42	-43	-44	-48	.0001			
100% machine flexibility, continuous tool delivery System								
ARF	16.7	9.12	10.8	5.6	0	NS	.009	NS
PRF	0				NS			
PMS	1.01	1.68	1.03	1.8	.003	0	.009	0
75% machine flexibility, limited tool magazine capacity								
ARF	6.83	9.34	19.8	2.5	NS	.036	.002	NS
PRF	4.63	4.81	12.4	2.3	NS	NS	.005	NS
CF	2.53	7.96	2.5	8.2	NS			
APMS	-1.2	3.05	3.2	3.2	NS			
INV	-35	-35	-33	-46	.001	0	0	0
75% Machine flexibility, continuous tool delivery system								
ARF	8.6	6.4	17.3	8.3	NS	.05	.001	NS
PRF	0				NS			
PMS	.65	.53	.64	1.1	NS	NS	.003	.001

ARF = Actual Routing Flexibility   PRF = Potential Routing Flexibility
CF = Capacity Flexibility   APMS = Adjusted Planned Makespan
PMS = Planned Makespan   INV = Inventory
NS = Not Significant   UNIF = Uniform Distribution
LTD = Left Triangular Distribution   RTD = Right Triangular Distribution
SUD = Symmetric Unimodal Distribution

That is, again the minimum cost policy has not only imparted a higher ARF but also has shown larger improvements with improvements in machine flexibility. However, the increase in planned makespan is higher with 100% machine flexibility than with lower machine flexibility. This is to be expected; when the machine flexibility is curtailed, the choices available also decreases. Consequently, both policies try to choose the very similar production routes, which is evident in the measure of ARF. An absolute convergence is expected in the case of the transfer line which has no flexibility.

The effect on inventory is very dominant with the maximum production rate policy resulting in higher inventory. However, this disadvantage is not at the benefit in capacity flexibility. The difference in capacity flexibility, although in favor of minimum cost policy, is not significant under both machine flexibility levels. In summary, it can be said that minimum cost policy imparts higher routing flexibility with marginal increase in capacity flexibility while resulting in low inventory. This is in essence efficient utilization of FMS.

Effects of Machine Flexibility on FMS Characteristics

Tables 6.11 and 6.12 represent the effect of machine flexibility on an FMS operating under one specified objective.

In the case of an FMS with continuous tool delivery system operating under the maximum production rate objective, when the machine flexibility decreases by 25% the planned makespan increases by as much as 17% as shown in Table 6.11. However, the routing flexibility decreases by as much as 13%. However, when the tool magazine capacity is limited, an increase in makespan ranges from 10% to 16% with no substantial decrease in routing flexibility. This is because this policy does not try to utilize the benefit of higher machine flexibility. The effect on capacity flexibility is more; it decreases by as much as 38%.

Under the minimum cost policy, the effect of machine flexibility is almost constant irrespective of part type distribution as shown in Table 6.12. With the continuous tool delivery system, the increase in makespan is around 16% with a decrease in routing flexibility around

Table 6.11: Effect of machine flexibility under maximum production rate policy.

System Characteristics	UNIF	LTD	RTD	SUD
With limited tool magazine capacity				
ARF	2.4 (NS)*	-.5 (NS)	-11 (S)	2.4 (NS)
PRF	.95 (NS)	0 (NS)	-8 (S)	-2 (NS)
CF	-34 (S)	-35 (S)	-38 (S)	-31 (S)
APMS	16 (S)	12 (S)	12 (S)	10 (S)
INV	-15 (NS)	-18 (NS)	-26 (S)	-3 (NS)
With continuous tool delivery system				
ARF	0 (NS)	-5 (NS)	-13 (S)	-8 (NS)
PRF	-1.4 (S)	-1.2 (S)	-1.5 (S)	-1.2 (S)
PMS	16.3 (S)	17 (S)	17 (S)	17 (S)

*The number is the percent increase for 75% machine flexibility, S means the increase is significant at least at .05 level, and NS means it is not significant.

UNIF = Uniform Distribution   SUD = Symmetric Unimodal
LTD = Left Triangular   RTD = Right Triangular
ARF = Actual Routing Flexibility   PMS = Planned Makespan
PRF = Potential "   "   CF = Capacity Flexibility
APMS = Adjusted Planned Makespan

Table 6.12: Effect of machine flexibility under minimum cost policy.

System Characteristics	UNIF	LTD	RTD	SUD
With limited tool magazine capacity				
ARF	-.6 (NS)*	-6 (NS)	-6 (NS)	-6 (NS)
PRF	1.7 (NS)	-.3 (NS)	1.4 (NS)	-1.4 (NS)
CF	-32 (S)	-34 (S)	-35 (S)	-28 (S)
APMS	15 (S)	14 (S)	17 (S)	12 (S)
With continuous tool delivery system				
ARF	-7 (S)	-8 (S)	-6 (S)	-8 (S)
PRF	-1.4 (S)	-1.2 (S)	-1.2 (S)	-1.4 (S)
PMS	15.8 (S)	16 (S)	16 (S)	17 (S)

*The number is the percent increase for 75% machine flexibility, S means the increase is significant at least at .05 level, and NS means it is not significant.

UNIF = Uniform Distribution   SUD = Symmetric Unimodal
LTD = Left Triangular   RTD = Right Triangular
ARF = Actual Routing Flexibility   PMS = Planned Makespan
PRF = Potential "   "   CF = Capacity Flexibility
APMS = Adjusted Planned Makespan

8%. Since this policy best utilizes the machine flexibility of FMS, the decrease in routing flexibility is not proportional to the decrease in machine flexibility. However, the decrease in capacity flexibility is more than the decrease in the machine flexibility but comparatively less compared to maximum production rate policy.

When the tool magazine capacity is limited, the makespan under minimum cost policy as shown in Table 6.12, increases in the range of 12% to 17% with a decrease in routing flexibility around 6%. Like before, the effect of machine flexibility is almost constant irrespective of part type distribution. From this it can be concluded that the minimum cost policy improves the performance of a FMS.

Effects of Tool Magazine Capacity on FMS Characteristics

The recent development in FMS technology, the continuous tool delivery system, virtually equips FMS with no limitation on tool magazine capacity. This renders FMS more flexible. The limitation on the tool magazine capacity often imposes batching of parts for simultaneous processing. Tables 6.13 and 6.14 capture the effects of the tool capacity level on FMS characteristics under both objectives.

The effects of the tool magazine capacity level on FMS characteristics are highly significant under both objectives for both 100% machine flexibility and 75% machine flexibility as shown in Tables 6.13 and 6.14. It is evident from the results that the effects are more pronounced for a 100% machine flexible FMS. This is to be expected. The reason is that as the machine flexibility decreases the effects should decrease. To see this consider the limiting case of machine flexibility, a transfer line. Since each operation can be performed on only one machine of a transfer line, the performance cannot be improved by providing unlimited tool magazine sizes.

Under the maximum production rate objective, as shown in Table 6.13, the ARF decreases by as much as 15.8%, PRF by 15.4%, and planned makespan increases by 18.3% in the case of 100% machine flexibility. But for the 75% machine flexibility, the effect is comparatively lower. The ARF decreases by as much as 11.2%, PRF by 19.0%, and planned makespan increases by 11.9%.

Table 6.13: Effect of tool magazine capacity under maximum production rate policy.

System Characteristics	UNIF	LTD	RTD	SUD
100% machine flexibility				
ARF	-9.7 (S)*	-15.8 (S)	-12.7 (S)	-15.1 (S)
PRF	-15.4 (S)	-13.4 (S)	-12.0 (S)	-12.2 (S)
PMS	12.5 (S)	17.0 (S)	15.5 (S)	18.3 (S)
75% machine flexibility				
ARF	-7.4 (S)	-11.2 (S)	-10.5 (S)	-5.7 (S)
PRF	-13.4 (S)	-19.0 (S)	-17.9 (S)	-12.7 (S)
PMS	11.7 (S)	11.9 (S)	10.6 (S)	11.3 (S)

*The number is the percent increase for limited tool magazine capacity and S means it is significant at least at .05 level.

UNIF = Uniform Distribution   SUD = Symmetric Unimodal
LTD = Left Triangular   RTD = Right Triangular
ARF = Actual Routing Flexibility   PMS = Planned Makespan
PRF = Potential "   "   CF = Capacity Flexibility

Table 6.14: Effect of tool magazine capacity under minimum cost policy.

System Characteristics	UNIF	LTD	RTD	SUD
100% machine flexibility				
ARF	-14.9 (S)[*]	-9.2 (S)	-10.5 (S)	-10.2 (S)
PRF	-12.1 (S)	-9.2 (S)	-10.4 (S)	-10.8 (S)
PMS	10.6 (S)	17.1 (S)	13.5 (S)	17.7 (S)
75% machine flexibility				
ARF	-8.9 (S)	-7.5 (S)	-8.5 (S)	-10.8 (S)
PRF	-9.3 (S)	-8.4 (S)	-7.8 (S)	-10.9 (S)
PMS	9.8 (S)	14.7 (S)	13.4 (S)	13.6 (S)

[*]The number is the percent increase for limited tool magazine capacity and S means it is significant at least at .05 level.

UNIF = Uniform Distribution   SUD = Symmetric Unimodal
LTD = Left Triangular   RTD = Right Triangular
ARF = Actual Routing Flexibility   PMS = Planned Makespan
PRF = Potential " "   CF = Capacity Flexibility

Under the minimum cost objective, as shown in Table 6.14, the ARF decreases by as much as 14.9%, PRF by 10.8%, and planned makespan increases by 17.7% in the case of 100% machine flexibility. For 75% machine flexibility, the effect is comparatively lower. The ARF decreases by as much as 10.8%, PRF by 10.9%, and planned makespan increases by 14.7%.

The important thing to note is the sensitivity of these measures to the tool capacity level across the four distributions. The maximum production rate objective is sensitive not only to tool capacity level but also for the distributions. The behavior of the minimum cost policy, on the other hand, is seen to be less sensitive. This is to be expected since the maximum production rate objective does not try to best utilize multiple production routes. Consequently, one may ask "Is there a loading and routing policy that yields acceptable system characteristics regardless of the demand distribution"? The results of Table 6.15 addresses this question.

Effects of Distributions on FMS characteristics

Although there is a relationship between the FMS characteristics, Table 6.15 lists only those that have high significance levels (below .05). Since the distributions are different, the t-test was performed only on the differences in the means.

Reduced sensitivity and higher stability imparts the greatest operational flexibility to the system (Gupta and Buzacott 1989). Sensitivity relates to the degree of change tolerated before performance degrades, and stability relates to the size of each disturbance for which the system can meet its expected performance level. In this study, sensitivity and stability are affected by part type distribution and their corresponding demand requirements. Thus, a policy that is fairly unaffected by the part type distribution is most suitable. From the results it is clear that the minimum cost policy meets those standards. Another question that becomes apparent is for which distribution the minimum cost policy should be derived. The choice from the simulation results is seen to be uniform distribution. Thus, a minimum cost policy derived for uniform distribution is most

Table 6.15: Effect of part type distribution.

Distribution	Minimum Cost Policy			Maximum Prod. Rate Policy		
	UNIF	RTD	SUD	UNIF	RTD	SUD
100% Machine flexibility, limited tool magazine capacity						
LTD	P*					
RTD			M,C			C
SUD	C	M,C			C	
100% machine flexibility, continuous tool delivery system						
LTD						
RTD			M,A,C			M,C
SUD	A,C	M,A,C			M,C	
75% Machine flexibility, limited tool magazine capacity						
LTD				I	A,I	
RTD			M,C	A,I		M,A ,C
SUD		M,C			M,A, C	
75% Machine flexibility, continuous tool delivery system						
LTD				I	A	
RTD			M,C	I		M,C
SUD		M,C			M,C	

* means significant (below .05) level.

UNIF = Uniform Distribution   SUD = Symmetric Unimodal
LTD = Left Triangular   RTD = Right Triangular
M = Planned Makespan   A = Actual Routing Flexibility
I = Inventory   P = Potential "   "
C = Capacity Flexibility

stable and less sensitive to changes in part type distribution and their quantities.

6.3 CONCLUSIONS ON HYPOTHESES TESTING

In this section, a summary of the results obtained under all four distributions is given. The testing procedures for each distribution were the same as discussed under uniform distribution.

Hypotheses Testing Related to Loading Policies

Table 6.10 shows the comparative improvement in FMS characteristics if a minimum cost policy is applied instead of a maximum production rate policy. Using the information in Table 6.10, the results of hypotheses testing related to loading policies is given in Table 6.16. In the following discussion, hypotheses 1 through 4 are discussed with respect to Table 6.16.

As regards to inventory, the minimum cost policy was found to reduce inventory compared to the maximum production rate policy. The results are statistically significant under all four distributions for both levels of machine flexibility.

Hypothesis 1, which implies minimum cost policy to result in relatively higher routing flexibility, was confirmed under uniform and right triangular distributions. It was not confirmed under symmetric unimodal distribution for a 100% machine flexible FMS, with or without any limitation on tool magazine capacity. However, under a left triangular distribution, this hypothesis was confirmed only when the tool magazine capacity was limited.

For a 75% machine flexible FMS, the conclusion for hypothesis 1 is same under both levels of tool magazine size. The hypothesis was confirmed only under left triangular and right triangular distributions. This means for a given distribution, the tool magazine limitation seems to have more effect on a 100% machine flexible FMS compared to a 75% machine flexible FMS. In addition, as the machine flexibility decreases, the performance difference in routing flexibility decreases. In all of the above cases, even when this

Table 6.16: Summary of results on hypotheses related to loading policies.

	Distribution	Hypothesis				
		INV	1	2	3	4
100% Mach. Flex. with limited tool magazine capacity	UNIF	S	S	NS		
	LTD	S	S	NS		S
	RTD	S	S	NS		
	SUD	S	NS	NS		S
100% Mach. Flex. continuous tool delivery system	UNIF	S	S	S	NS	
	LTD	S	NS	S	NS	
	RTD	S	S	S	NS	
	SUD	S	NS	S	NS	
75% Mach. Flex. with limited tool magazine capacity	UNIF	S	NS	NS		
	LTD	S	S	NS		
	RTD	S	S	NS		
	SUD	S	NS	NS		S
75% Mach. Flex. continuous tool delivery system	UNIF	S	NS	NS		
	LTD	S	S	NS		
	RTD	S	S	S	NS	
	SUD	S	NS	S	NS	

S = Supported   RTD = Right Triangular Distribution
NS = Not Supported   LTD = Left Triangular Distribution
INV = Inventory   UNIF = Uniform Distribution
  SUD = Symmetric Unimodal Distribution

hypothesis was not confirmed, the minimum cost policy still imparted comparatively higher routing flexibility.

Hypothesis 2, which expresses maximum production rate policy to result in a comparatively lower planned makespan, was not confirmed under both machine flexibility levels when the tool magazine capacity is limited. However, when the tool magazine size is unlimited, this hypothesis was confirmed under all distributions in the case of 100% machine flexibility. In the case of 75% machine flexibility, this hypothesis was confirmed only under right triangular and symmetric unimodal distributions.

Hypothesis 3, which purports the maximum production rate policy to result in comparatively higher capacity flexibility, was not confirmed under all distributions for both levels of machine flexibility.

Hypothesis 4, which states the maximum production rate policy to result in comparatively fewer part groups, was only confirmed in three cases, under both machine flexibility levels for symmetric unimodal distribution, and for left triangular distribution under 100% machine flexibility case.

Hypotheses Testing Related to Machine Flexibility

Table 6.17 shows the results of hypotheses testing related to machine flexibility. This table is developed using the information of Tables 6.11 and 6.12. In the following discussion, hypotheses 5 through 8 are discussed with respect to Table 6.17.

Hypothesis 5, which implies lower machine flexibility to result in comparatively higher makespan, was confirmed for all distributions under both loading policies for an FMS with or without any limitation on the tool magazine capacity.

Hypothesis 6, which implies lower machine flexibility to result in comparatively lower capacity flexibility, was confirmed for all distributions under both loading policies.

Hypothesis 7, which expresses lower machine flexibility to impart relatively lower routing flexibility, was not confirmed under minimum cost policy when the tool magazine capacity is limited. However, when the tool magazine capacity was unlimited, this hypothesis was supported. Under the maximum production rate policy,

Table 6.17: Summary of results on hypotheses related to machine flexibility.

Hypothesis	Loading objective	Distribution			
		UNIF	LTD	RTD	SUD
FMS with limited tool magazine capacity					
5	Min. Cost	S	S	S	S
	Max. Prod.	S	S	S	S
6	Min. Cost	S	S	S	S
	Max. Prod.	S	S	S	S
7	Min. Cost	NS	NS	NS	NS
	Max. Prod.	NS	NS	S	NS
8	Max. Prod.	NS	NS	NS	NS
FMS with continuous tool delivery system					
5	Min. Cost	S	S	S	S
	Max. Prod.	S	S	S	S
6	Min. cost	S	S	S	S
	Max. Prod.	S	S	S	S
7	Min. Cost	S	S	S	S
	Max. Prod.	NS	NS	S	NS
8	Max. Prod.	NS	NS	NS	NS

S = Supported
NS = Not Supported

UNIF = Uniform Distribution
LTD = Left Triangular Distribution
RTD = Right Triangular Distribution
SUD = Symmetric Uniform Distribution

the results are identical for both levels of tool magazine capacity. The hypothesis was confirmed only for a right triangular distribution.

Hypothesis 8, which expresses lower machine flexibility to carry relatively lower inventory, was not confirmed under all distributions. Although the results are not statistically significant, they favor the hypothesis.

It should be noted that to elicit the effects of loading policies, machine flexibility, and tool magazine capacity separately on FMS characteristics, paired difference tests were performed. Since only one parameter was allowed to vary the testing procedure is perfectly valid. It was needed since the hypotheses were based on two factors: loading policies, and machine flexibility. However, analysis of variance test (ANOVA) can be performed to simultaneously study the effects of the above parameters on the FMS performance. This is not pursued in this study but will be reported elsewhere.

VII

Study Implications

In the previous chapter, the results of hypotheses tests, together with the effects of FMS hardware constraints on system characteristics, were presented. In this chapter, implications for management are provided along with extensions. Managerial implications are provided in Section 7.1. Extensions are given in Section 7.2

7.1 IMPLICATIONS FOR MANAGEMENT

The results of this study are general in scope because the FMS configuration used and the random selection of the input data pertain to a typical FMS that is found in practice. The FMS configured in this research is based on the findings of Ito (1987), Sarin and Chen (1987), Mortimer (1984), Kochan (1984), Lashkari et al. (1987), Smith et al. (1986), Shanker and Tzen (1985), and Edghill and Creswell (1985). The range of utilization of the FMS in this research is from 49% to 91.4%. This is in accordance with the survey results of Smith et al. (1986). The simulated demand imposed variable requirements on the FMS over the planning horizon. Hence, the results are robust in that they were obtained from analyzing many replications of the short run requirements of the FMS.

As such, the flexibility measures developed represent the ability of an existing system to respond to disturbances. These measures are sensitivity measures in that they represent the bounds on the disturbances beyond which the system would not be able to respond. The higher the bounds, or the flexibility measures, the larger the disturbances the system can handle. The following implications are drawn from this study.

Implications Related to Loading Policies

1. The minimum cost policy results in significantly lower inventory compared to a maximum production rate policy.

2. The minimum cost policy imparts higher actual routing flexibility (ARF) to an FMS compared to maximum production rate policy. This is consistent across all four distributions and at both levels of machine flexibility and tool magazine capacity. Further, for a given machine flexibility and tool magazine capacity, the minimum cost policy is observed to impart higher ARF as the production demand imposed on FMS decreases. As the demand increases, the difference in ARF decreases, which is to be expected.

3. An FMS with a continuous tool delivery system has the same potential routing flexibility (PRF) under both loading policies at both levels of machine flexibility. However, as the tool magazine capacity decreases, the minimum cost policy imparts higher PRF than the maximum production rate policy.

4. The planned makespan is higher under minimum cost policy than the maximum production rate policy. The differences are statistically significant for an FMS with 100% machine flexibility. However, as the machine flexibility decreases, the difference in the planned makespan also decreases. This is to be expected.

5. The results favor a minimum cost policy, even though the differences in capacity flexibility between the two policies are not significant. As production demand decreases, the minimum cost policy creates more capacity flexibility than the maximum production rate policy. This is true for both levels of flexibility. Besides, as machine flexibility decreases, the minimum cost policy was found to impart relatively higher capacity flexibility compared to the maximum production rate policy. This result is noteworthy, because most FMS's are not fully flexible. Thus, the benefits of a minimum cost policy cannot be overlooked.

6. The minimum cost policy results in a higher number of part groups than the maximum production rate policy. However, this is not a drawback. The differences are not statistically significant.

Implications Related to FMS Hardware Constraints

1. The effect of the tool magazine capacity on FMS characteristics is significant under both planning policies at both levels of machine flexibility. Actual routing flexibility and potential routing flexibility decrease as tool magazine capacity decreases. The planned makespan increases. The effect is more pronounced for a 100 % machine flexible FMS than for a 75% machine flexible FMS.
2. Machine flexibility has pronounced effects on the planned makespan, ARF, PRF, and CF for an FMS with a continuous tool delivery system. As machine flexibility decreases, the planned makespan increases, while ARF, PRF, and CF decreases. However, in the case of limited tool magazine capacity, these effects are not statistically significant. Only the planned makespan was found to increase significantly.
3. The above result implies that if there is limited tool magazine capacity, lower machine flexibility can be partly compensated for by the increased routing flexibility.
4. When the tool magazine is limited, the difference between loading policies with respect to the planned makespan increases as machine flexibility decreases. That is, the effect of tool magazine capacity becomes more prominent as machine flexibility decreases.
5. As machine flexibility decreases for an FMS with limited tool magazine capacity, the ARF resulting from the minimum cost policy approaches the ARF of the maximum production rate policy.
6. As machine flexibility decreases for an FMS with limited tool magazine capacity, the number of part groups required by the minimum cost policy approaches the number of part groups required by the maximum production rate policy.
7. Changes in machine flexibility do not proportionally affect the FMS system characteristics. The percentage changes are greater for the maximum production rate policy than the minimum cost policy.

The foregoing implications indicate that the minimum cost policy not only imparts greater flexibility to an FMS for a given machine flexibility but also allows for larger improvements in flexibility as the machine flexibility increases.

From the results of the previous chapter, it can be said that the maximum production rate policy is sensitive to both the tool capacity level and to the   distribution of production demand. Whereas, the minimum cost policy is less sensitive. Gupta and Buzacott (1989) note that reduced sensitivity imparts greater flexibility to an FMS. Consequently, the minimum cost policy is better suited as a planning objective for an FMS than the maximum production rate policy.

7.2 DIRECTION FOR FUTURE STUDIES

Although the flexibility measures derived in this study and the minimum cost LRM model show promise, they raise questions for future research. They are:

1. The flexibility is a multi-dimensional concept. Can flexibility measures be combined in a meaningful way to obtain one measure for overall system flexibility that is consistent with decision making and not just a combination of numerical values?
2. Flexibility measures can be used as objectives in tool loading and part routing decisions. What is the effect of using flexibility measures as objectives in the production planning process?
3. Because the minimum cost LRM model has been shown to increase flexibility, can efficient and effective heuristics can be found to allow firms to easily apply the minimum cost policy?
4. Would the benefit of the minimum cost policy continue to persist after scheduling? What are the best dispatching rules for each policy? Are they different?
5. How do these policies compare with each other in terms of tool consumption and tool inventory? How susceptible or sensitive is each policy to tool management?

Cox (1989), in a study of manufacturing strategies, reports that the flexibility was ranked first in the size of the strategic gap. That is, the difference between current capability and future flexibility needs is perceived to be the largest area for improvement. If his findings are accepted, then the above questions must be addressed and answered relative to their decision making impact.

Appendices

Appendix A

This appendix contains the results of simulation runs. Against each run, the performance measures are given. In the following tables, Eta denotes FMS utilization, MS denotes makespan, CF represents capacity flexibility, and ARF and PRF represent actual and potential routing flexibilities, respectively.

Run	Qty	Eta	CF	Inv	Lim. Tool Mag.			Cont. Tool Del.		
					MS	ARF	PRF	MS	ARF	PR F
1	309	.509	1.72		2596	.687	.852	2198	.75	.95
2	327	.506	1.56		2298	.67	.849	2185	.70	.96
3	416	.679	.855		3203	.589	.885	2933	.717	.96
4	477	.738	.609		3520	.539	.851	3187	.706	.96
5	479	.784	.50		3896	.557	.848	3388	.721	.96
6	348	.544	1.38		2564	.641	.875	2348	.744	.96
7	368	.606	1.16		2833	.648	.788	2617	.749	.96
8	323	.548	1.29		2498	.604	.857	2369	.675	.97
9	359	.571	1.25		2715	.640	.778	2468	.755	.97
10	446	.723	.695		3520	.544	.856	3123	.670	.96
Avg	385	0.62	1.10		2964	0.61	0.84	2681	0.72	.96

Table A.1: Results for 100% Design Flexibility Under Uniform Distribution With Minimum Cost Policy.

Run	Qty	Eta	CF	Inv	Lim. Tool Mag.			Cont. Tool Del.		
					MS	ARF	PRF	MS	ARF	PRF
1	309	.561	1.27		2840	.638	.886	2421	.704	.94
2	327	.590	1.05		2936	.710	.874	2548	.710	.94
3	416	.777	.538		3628	.542	.787	3358	.595	.95
4	477	.867	.284		4111	.570	.881	3745	.624	.94
5	479	.910	.188		4269	.546	.871	3931	.591	.94
6	348	.617	1.09		2797	.626	.906	2666	.706	.95
7	368	.710	.754		3237	.690	.787	3065	.711	.95
8	323	.686	.893		3237	.634	.874	2964	.685	.95
9	359	.623	1.08		2980	.549	.836	2693	.677	.96
10	446	.849	.343		4062	.584	.880	3668	.675	.95
Avg	385	0.72	0.75		3409	0.61	0.86	3106	0.67	.95

Table A.2: Results for 75% Design Flexibility Under Uniform Distribution With Minimum Cost Policy.

Run	Qty	Eta	CF	Inv	Lim. Tool Mag.			Cont. Tool Del.		
					MS	ARF	PRF	MS	ARF	PRF
1	309	.496	1.55	160	2535	.665	.871	2142	.748	.95
2	327	.508	1.63	253	2396	.55	.775	2194	.60	.96
3	416	.671	.876	101	3501	.509	.864	2899	.612	.96
4	477	.737	.613	135	3387	.539	.787	3183	.579	.96
5	479	.782	.502	169	4117	.464	.886	3378	.541	.96
6	348	.530	1.44	102	2664	.620	.871	2291	.698	.96
7	368	.598	1.20	181	2701	.574	.755	2581	.574	.96
8	323	.541	1.35	131	2584	.536	.748	2335	.576	.97
9	359	.567	1.27	247	2448	.636	.758	2448	.636	.97
10	446	.717	.703	145	3528	.470	.808	3096	.596	.96
Avg	3850	0.61	1.11	162	2986	0.56	0.81	2654	0.62	.96

Table A.3: Results for 100% Design Flexibility Under Uniform Distribution With Maximum Production Rate Policy.

Run	Qty	Eta	CF	Inv	Lim. Tool Mag.			Cont. Tool Del.		
					MS	ARF	PRF	MS	ARF	PR F
1	309	.558	1.22	126	2531	.446	.676	2410	.481	.94
2	327	.589	1.14	266	2895	.595	.821	2531	.670	.94
3	416	.779	.538	70	3744	.593	.815	3367	.676	.95
4	477	.866	.288	78	3948	.535	.806	3739	.558	.94
5	479	.914	.186	35	4370	.485	.839	3948	.549	.95
6	348	.612	.985	117	2833	.580	.806	2645	.622	.94
7	368	.710	.754	140	3636	.768	.891	3065	.774	.95
8	323	.656	.882	240	3563	.612	.844	2833	.658	.96
9	359	.620	.959	234	2989	.567	.830	2680	.603	.96
10	446	.847	.349	79	3983	.516	.871	3659	.560	.95
Avg	385	0.72	0.73	138	3449	0.57	0.82	3087	0.62	.95

Table A.4: Results for 75% Design Flexibility Under Uniform Distribution With Maximum Production Rate Objective.

Run	Qty	Eta	CF	Inv	Lim. Tool Mag.			Cont. Tool Del.		
					MS	ARF	PRF	MS	ARF	PR F
1	368	.630	1.02		3225	.525	.885	2720	.697	.97
2	288	.493	1.67		2435	.612	.839	2131	.686	.95
3	408	.646	.943		3399	.539	.837	2789	.679	.96
4	379	.620	.972		3364	.660	.886	2680	.768	.97
5	331	.576	1.24		2748	.754	.861	2487	.777	.96
6	363	.607	1.07		3036	.658	.838	2623	.706	.96
7	360	.609	1.19		2861	.708	.858	2629	.722	.96
8	303	.482	1.86		2280	.706	.922	2080	.767	.96
9	326	.519	1.43		2601	.728	.904	2242	.728	.96
10	352	.648	.935		3541	.607	.902	2797	.626	.97
Avg	348	0.58	1.23		2949	0.65	0.87	2518	0.72	.96

Table A.5: Results for 100% Design Flexibility Under Left Triangular Distribution With Minimum Cost Policy.

Run	Qty	Eta	CF	Inv	Lim. Tool Mag.			Cont. Tool Del.		
					MS	ARF	PRF	MS	ARF	PR F
1	368	.730	.675		3497	.581	.861	3154	.683	.96
2	288	.561	1.10		2584	.592	.748	2423	.592	.94
3	408	.774	.505		3814	.589	.876	3343	.675	.95
4	379	.745	.562		3755	.637	.894	3216	.665	.96
5	331	.656	.828		3158	.637	.876	2834	.637	.95
6	363	.697	.729		3700	.618	.904	3012	.707	.94
7	360	.689	.795		3486	.537	.870	2978	.651	.95
8	303	.548	1.43		2616	.574	.902	2365	.617	.95
9	326	.625	.998		3100	.639	.883	2698	.638	.95
10	352	.732	.545		3776	.680	.889	3161	.711	.96
Avg	348	0.68	0.82		3348	0.61	0.87	2918	0.66	.95

Table A.6: Results for 75% Design Flexibility Under Left Triangular Distribution With Minimum Cost Policy.

Run	Qty	Eta	CF	Inv	Lim. Tool Mag.			Cont. Tool Del.		
					MS	ARF	PRF	MS	ARF	PR F
1	368	.626	1.06	79	3074	.521	.845	2705	.655	.97
2	288	.490	1.63	64	2472	.611	.780	2115	.703	.95
3	408	.640	.960	158	3030	.501	.828	2756	.579	.96
4	379	.613	.815	130	3073	.541	.777	2646	.612	.97
5	331	.559	1.23	175	2955	.475	.847	2413	.606	.96
6	363	.595	1.04	214	2891	.453	.839	2569	.569	.96
7	360	.593	1.06	202	3262	.587	.875	2563	.734	.96
8	303	.465	1.89	135	2144	.480	.796	2015	.629	.96
9	326	.511	1.11	167	2643	.651	.826	2209	.709	.96
10	352	.642	.770	177	3419	.719	.913	2772	.780	.97
Avg	348	0.57	1.16	150	2896	0.55	0.83	2476	0.66	.96

Table A.7: Results for 100% Design Flexibility Under Left
Triangular Distribution With Maximum Production Rate Policy.

Run	Qty	Eta	CF	Inv	Lim. Tool Mag.			Cont. Tool Del.		
					MS	ARF	PRF	MS	ARF	PR F
1	368	.720	.724	100	3513	.556	.835	3111	.609	.96
2	288	.557	1.00	139	2811	.567	.885	2407	.645	.94
3	408	.769	.485	172	3537	.464	.885	3320	.615	.95
4	379	.746	.502	68	3594	.533	.816	3222	.639	.96
5	331	.651	.764	178	3189	.545	.710	2812	.619	.95
6	363	.693	.748	105	3335	.639	.859	2994	.684	.95
7	360	.685	.795	64	3470	.594	.832	2959	.679	.95
8	303	.535	1.36	123	2557	.562	.864	2313	.606	.95
9	326	.619	.636	192	2901	.577	.758	2675	.640	.95
10	352	.745	.528	88	3589	.531	.877	3217	.531	.96
Avg	348	0.67	0.75	123	3249	0.56	0.83	2903	0.63	.95

Table A.8: Results for 75% Design Flexibility Under Left
Triangular Distribution With Maximum Production Rate Policy.

Run	Qty	Eta	CF	Inv	Lim. Tool Mag.			Cont. Tool Del.		
					MS	ARF	PRF	MS	ARF	PR F
1	300	.502	1.48		2499	.664	.927	2170	.715	.98
2	348	.602	1.18		3059	.744	.934	2599	.771	.97
3	394	.658	.968		3299	.652	.844	2840	.755	.97
4	424	.701	.753		3452	.620	.856	3030	.727	.96
5	412	.636	.902		2995	.675	.886	2749	.742	.96
6	423	.675	.824		3266	.554	.847	2914	.670	.96
7	408	.664	.924		3369	.606	.808	2868	.706	.96
8	360	.563	1.30		2663	.622	.867	2434	.692	.96
9	365	.584	1.23		2805	.722	.846	2521	.722	.96
10	509	.813	.404		3951	.554	.835	3510	.661	.96
Avg	394	0.64	1.00		3136	0.64	0.87	2763	0.72	.96

Table A.9: Results for 100% Design Flexibility Under Right Triangular Distribution With Minimum Cost Policy.

Run	Qty	Eta	CF	Inv	Lim. Tool Mag.			Cont. Tool Del.		
					MS	ARF	PRF	MS	ARF	PR F
1	300	.584	1.11		2830	.533	.889	2521	.647	.96
2	348	.719	.755		3704	.605	.893	3106	.626	.96
3	394	.760	.622		3824	.673	.912	3283	.708	.96
4	424	.818	.434		3921	.599	.865	3533	.675	.95
5	412	.740	.642		3440	.647	.888	3194	.646	.95
6	423	.786	.512		3896	.506	.875	3394	.618	.95
7	408	.764	.588		3832	.624	.886	3299	.647	.94
8	360	.676	.767		3350	.566	.865	2922	.685	.94
9	365	.655	.956		3147	.639	.836	2831	.673	.95
10	509	.957	.094		4601	.643	.862	4134	.670	.95
Avg	394	0.75	0.65		3654	0.60	0.88	3222	0.66	.95

Table A.10: Results for 75% Design Flexibility Under Right
Triangular Distribution With Minimum Cost Policy.

Run	Qty	Eta	CF	Inv	Lim. Tool Mag.			Cont. Tool Del.		
					MS	ARF	PRF	MS	ARF	PRF
1	300	.496	1.39	149	2547	.602	.907	2141	.686	.98
2	348	.593	1.21	192	2773	.470	.791	2562	.565	.97
3	394	.645	.981	176	3279	.551	.879	2788	.652	.97
4	424	.693	.765	72	3571	.600	.817	2994	.670	.96
5	412	.627	.996	262	3237	.509	.874	2709	.637	.96
6	423	.678	.852	136	3299	.535	.814	2927	.621	.96
7	408	.663	.931	147	3069	.524	.829	2863	.584	.96
8	360	.557	1.33	247	2915	.657	.867	2406	.696	.96
9	365	.566	1.28	220	2749	.677	.812	2447	.690	.96
10	509	.814	.402	124	4155	.526	.890	3517	.669	.96
Avg	394	0.63	1.01	172	3159	0.57	0.85	2735	0.65	.96

Table A.11: Results for 100% Design Flexibility Under Right Triangular Distribution With Maximum Production Rate Policy.

Run	Qty	Eta	CF	Inv	Lim. Tool Mag.			Cont. Tool Del.		
					MS	ARF	PRF	MS	ARF	PRF
1	300	.586	.966	109	3015	.502	.881	2529	.595	.96
2	348	.712	.689	126	3646	.558	.901	3076	.576	.96
3	394	.753	.633	90	3602	.529	.841	3251	.529	.96
4	424	.815	.446	22	3790	.555	.735	3521	.635	.95
5	412	.731	.666	140	3556	.552	.674	3156	.586	.95
6	423	.786	.510	57	3637	.474	.782	3394	.596	.95
7	408	.761	.595	203	3288	.433	.651	3288	.433	.94
8	360	.669	.851	259	3217	.500	.818	2891	.581	.95
9	365	.646	.874	190	3172	.519	.695	2792	.595	.95
10	509	.952	.094	85	4484	.413	.826	4113	.496	.95
Avg	394	0.74	0.63	128	3541	0.50	0.78	3201	0.56	.95

Table A.12: Results for 75% Design Flexibility Under Right Triangular Distribution With Maximum Production Rate Policy.

Run	Qty	Eta	CF	Inv	Lim. Tool Mag.			Cont. Tool Del.		
					MS	ARF	PRF	MS	ARF	PRF
1	380	.668	.857		3345	.575	.839	2884	.734	.98
2	331	.534	1.44		2578	.604	.830	2305	.635	.97
3	352	.560	1.37		2725	.670	.828	2419	.684	.97
4	395	.622	1.03		3008	.588	.886	2687	.644	.96
5	333	.558	1.43		2977	.617	.902	2410	.678	.96
6	331	.510	1.63		2448	.595	.842	2204	.675	.95
7	284	.457	1.95		2468	.588	.859	1976	.714	.97
8	284	.512	1.79		2883	.646	.862	2212	.672	.97
9	367	.589	1.21		2941	.648	.858	2546	.722	.96
10	284	.494	1.84		2609	.620	.898	2135	.690	.96
Avg	334	0.55	1.45		2798	0.62	0.86	2378	0.68	.97

Table A.13: Results for 100% Design Flexibility Under Symmetric Unimodal Distribution With Minimum Cost Policy.

Run	Qty	Eta	CF	Inv	Lim. Tool Mag.			Cont. Tool Del.		
					MS	ARF	PRF	MS	ARF	PR F
1	380	.768	.547		3741	.521	.873	3319	.666	.96
2	331	.618	1.03		3206	.519	.767	2668	.613	.96
3	352	.663	.971		3121	.552	.865	2863	.616	.96
4	395	.741	.602		3695	.660	.877	3201	.737	.95
5	333	.642	.963		3021	.552	.749	2772	.612	.95
6	331	.599	1.18		3001	.579	.897	2586	.651	.94
7	284	.524	1.62		2585	.529	.894	2264	.625	.96
8	284	.549	1.45		2700	.635	.828	2372	.635	.96
9	367	.720	.691		3492	.584	.866	3108	.617	.95
10	284	.564	1.41		2781	.633	.870	2436	.687	.95
Avg	334	0.64	1.05		3134	0.58	0.85	2759	0.65	.95

Table A.14: Results for 75% Design Flexibility Under Symmetric Unimodal Distribution With Minimum Cost Policy.

Run	Qty	Eta	CF	Inv	Lim. Tool Mag.			Cont. Tool Del.		
					MS	ARF	PRF	MS	ARF	PR F
1	380	.663	.955	86	3697	.680	.870	2862	.779	.98
2	331	.520	1.20	189	2415	.542	.853	2246	.636	.97
3	352	.550	1.41	195	2903	.518	.863	2373	.602	.97
4	395	.610	1.08	206	2946	.558	.824	2645	.663	.96
5	333	.550	1.31	204	2952	.654	.870	2387	.735	.96
6	331	.500	1.64	140	2339	.480	.806	2173	.610	.95
7	284	.450	1.75	145	2151	.683	.849	1933	.708	.97
8	284	.500	1.67	177	2451	.365	.794	2150	.492	.97
9	367	.580	1.12	154	3127	.505	.881	2494	.618	.96
10	284	.490	1.92	98	2661	.520	.862	2106	.644	.96
Avg	334	0.54	1.41	159	2764	0.55	0.85	2337	0.65	.97

Table A.15: Results for 100% Design Flexibility Under Symmetric Unimodal Distribution With Maximum Production Rate Policy.

Run	Qty	Eta	CF	Inv	Lim. Tool Mag.			Cont. Tool Del.		
					MS	ARF	PRF	MS	ARF	PRF
1	380	.770	.613	127	3714	.612	.888	3310	.668	.96
2	331	.610	.825	180	2886	.656	.915	2647	.656	.96
3	352	.660	.883	208	3189	.403	.890	2851	.535	.95
4	395	.733	.660	124	3262	.592	.713	3165	.374	.95
5	333	.629	.885	209	3296	.461	.749	2716	.580	.95
6	331	.598	1.12	107	2685	.570	.816	2581	.570	.94
7	284	.515	1.33	209	2663	.573	.801	2225	.672	.96
8	284	.542	1.31	129	2621	.629	.873	2342	.681	.96
9	367	.712	.675	56	3550	.560	.862	3077	.601	.95
10	284	.553	1.41	194	2508	.575	.792	2387	.633	.95
Avg	334	0.63	0.97	154	3037	0.56	0.83	2730	0.60	.95

Table A.16: Results for 75% Design Flexibility Under Symmetric Unimodal Distribution With Maximum Production Rate Policy.

Appendix B

This appendix contains a fortran program for analyzing the LRM output to determine if the part grouping is necessary. Part grouping will be required if the total tool assignment to any of the five machines exceed its tool magazine capacity which in this research is 5 tool slots. A output from this program is given.

```
        CHARACTER RA*3,RD*6,RC*3,RB*14
        DIMENSION  X(811),L(5,3),M(5,3),MF(5,3),IX(811)
        OPEN(UNIT=10, FILE='/MMINZ06 SOL',STATUS='OLD')
        READ(10,14)
        READ(10,15)(X(I),I=1,811)
15      FORMAT(24X,F10.5,38X)
14      FORMAT(72X)
        CLOSE(UNIT=10, STATUS='KEEP')
        DO 1 IT=1,3
        DO 2 K=1,5
        L(K,IT)=0
        M(K,IT)=0
        MF(K,IT)=0
2       CONTINUE
1       CONTINUE
        DO 17 I=1,811
        IX(I)=INT(X(I))
17      CONTINUE
        I=366
        J=381
        DO 5 IT=1,3
        DO 7 K=1,5
        IF(IX(I).GT.0.AND.IX(I+10).GT.0)  L(K,IT)=1
        IF(IX(I).GT.0.AND.IX(I+70).GT.0)  L(K,IT)=1
        IF(IX(I+10).GT.0.AND.IX(I+70).GT.0)  L(K,IT) = 1
        IF(IX(I).GT.0.AND.IX(I+10).GT.0.AND.IX(I+70).GT.0)  L(K,IT)=2
        IF(IX(J).GT.0.AND.IX(J+70).GT.0)  M(K,IT)=1
        IF(IX(J).GT.0.AND.IX(J+85).GT.0)  M(K,IT)=1
        IF(IX(J+70).GT.0.AND.IX(J+85).GT.0)  M(K,IT) = 1
        IF(IX(J).GT.0.AND.IX(J+70).GT.0.AND.IX(J+85).GT.0)  M(K,IT)=2
        I=I+1
        J=J+1
7       CONTINUE
        I=I+115
        J=J+115
5       CONTINUE
        DO 37 IT=1,3
        DO 37 K=1,5
        MF(K,IT)=0
```

135

```
37        CONTINUE
          II=361
          III=476
          DO 50 IT=1,3
          DO 55 K=1,5
          DO 60 I = II,III,5
          IF(IX(I).LE.0) GO TO 60
          MF(K,IT)=MF(K,IT)+IX(I-360)
60        CONTINUE
          MF(K,IT)=MF(K,IT)-L(K,IT)-M(K,IT)
       WRITE(*,90)IT,K,MF(K,IT)
90    FORMAT(5X,'PERIOD',I2,2X,'MACHINE',I2,'# OF TOOLS',2X,I2)
          II=II+1
          III=III+1
55        CONTINUE
          II=III
          III=III+115
       WRITE(*,*)
       WRITE(*,*)
50        CONTINUE
          STOP
          END
```

The output from this program is:

```
PERIOD 1  MACHINE 1  # OF TOOLS  6
PERIOD 1  MACHINE 2  # OF TOOLS  5
PERIOD 1  MACHINE 3  # OF TOOLS  3
PERIOD 1  MACHINE 4  # OF TOOLS  6
PERIOD 1  MACHINE 5  # OF TOOLS  5

         TOTAL BATCHES REQUIRED = 2

PERIOD 2  MACHINE 1  # OF TOOLS  7
PERIOD 2  MACHINE 2  # OF TOOLS  5
PERIOD 2  MACHINE 3  # OF TOOLS  5
PERIOD 2  MACHINE 4  # OF TOOLS  8
PERIOD 2  MACHINE 5  # OF TOOLS  6

         TOTAL BATCHES REQUIRED = 2

PERIOD 3  MACHINE 1  # OF TOOLS  8
PERIOD 3  MACHINE 2  # OF TOOLS  5
PERIOD 3  MACHINE 3  # OF TOOLS  6
PERIOD 3  MACHINE 4  # OF TOOLS  7
PERIOD 3  MACHINE 5  # OF TOOLS  6

         TOTAL BATCHES REQUIRED = 2
```

Appendix C

This appendix contains mathematical formulation for calculating the capacity flexibility. Capacity flexibility is calculated after LRM is solved.

$$Maximize \quad CF = \sum_t \frac{\sum_i D_{it}}{\sum_t \sum_i D_{it}} \sum_i CF_{it} \frac{D_{it}}{\sum_i D_{it}}$$

$$\sum_i \sum_j P_{ijk} \, n_{ijkt} \leq 1440 - MS_t + S_{tk} \qquad \forall \ i,j,k,t$$

$$\sum_k n_{ijkt} = Q_{it} \qquad \forall \ i,j,t$$

$$\frac{Q_{it}}{D_{it}} = CF_{it} \qquad \forall \ i,t$$

$$n_{ijkt} \geq 0 \ (integer)$$

where :

CF_{it} = *Capacity Flexibility of part i in period t*
Q_{it} = *Extra units of part i that can be produced*
MS_t = *Makespan in period t LRM*
S_{tk} = *Slack of machine k in period t*
D_{it} = *Demand of part i in period t*
n_{ijkt} = *# of units of part i done on mach. k in per. t*
P_{ijk} = *Proc. time of opn. j of part i on mach. k*

Appendix D

This appendix contains the computer program to calculate the actual routing flexibility and potential routing flexibility. Algorithm on which this fortran program is based is given along with a typical output.

Algorithm for Actual and Potential Routing Flexibility

For the part types chosen for simultaneous processing in a period do the following:

1. Analyze and store for each part type its machine - operation assignment and update this information to make use of common tooling.
2. Calculate the actual routing flexibility for each part type based on the measure developed earlier.
3. For each machine find the number of empty tool slots.
4. For each part type chosen assign empty tool slots according to weight calculated as a ratio of its demand to total demand of part types selected for concurrent production.
5. For each part type, to maximize the routing flexibility, assign a tool (slot) to that operation that has least number of machine assignments. Assign this operation to a machine to which it has not been assigned and is feasible. The feasibility complication arises in the case of 75% design flexibility. In that case machines are scanned to see the feasibility of assignment if possible. In case of no possibility, next operation with least number of assignments is chosen and the procedure is repeated.
6. Repeat step 5 for each part type.
7. If some tool slots are left free after steps 5 and 6, because of restriction, then assign these tool slots to part types weighted according to its number of operations to total number of operations in that batch.

139

8.   Repeat steps 5 and 6 until all free slots are assigned or after certain number of loops which may be necessary in the case of 75% design flexibility.

9.   Update machine - operation assignment and benefit from any common tooling for all part types.

10.   Calculate the potential routing flexibility for each part type based on the measure given before.

11.   Calculate the aggregate measure of actual and potential routing flexibility based on the aggregate measure provided in Chapter II.

The Computer Program

```
        *************************************************************
C
C            THIS PROGRAM CALCULATES ROUTING FLEXIBILITY FOR
C            PERIOD 1. SIMILAR PROGRAM HAS TO BE REPEATED FOR
C            OTHER PERIODS.
C
C        *************************************************************
C
        IMPLICIT INTEGER (I-N)
        COMMON AL(811),PT(24,5),MFTS(5),IPRAS(8,5),MFSLTS
        DIMENSION IND(8),NOFOP(8),IPS(8),ISP(8),IEP(8)
        DIMENSION IPR(8),ITAR(8),MTS(5),LA(5),MA(5),ITS(8),QP(8),DI(8)
C     INPUT DATA STATEMENTS
C       DATA(IPS(I),I=1,8)/1,1,0,1,0,1,0,0/
        DATA(ISP(I),I=1,8)/361,376,381,391,406,426,451,461/
        DATA(IEP(I),I=1,8)/371,376,386,401,421,446,456,476/
        DATA(IND(I),I=1,8)/1,4,5,7,10,14,19,21/
        DATA(NOFOP(I),I=1,8)/3,1,2,3,4,5,2,4/
C     FINISH DATA STATEMENTS
C
C     OPENING THE FILES TO READ MACHINE PROCESSING TIMES AND
C     THE OUTPUT FILES FROM MODEL LRM.
C
        OPEN(UNIT=5, FILE = '/MCTIMFF DATA', STATUS = 'OLD')
        READ (5,*)((PT(I,J),J=1,5),I=1,24)
        CLOSE(UNIT=5, STATUS= 'KEEP')
C     OPENING A FILE FOR OUTPUT
        OPEN(UNIT=10, FILE = '/PFMINT14 SOL',STATUS ='OLD')
        READ(10,11)
        READ(10,12)(AL(I),I=1,811)
   11   FORMAT(72X)
   12   FORMAT(24X,F10.5,38X)
```

```
C      CLOSE(UNIT=10, STATUS = 'KEEP')
C
       CALL LRMREAD(AL)
C      FINISH READING OUTPUT AND M/C TIMES.
C
C      CALCULATE TOTAL QUANTITY PRODUCED
C
       TQPR=0.0
       DO 7 I = 1,8
       IPS(I)=0
       IF(AL(I+744).GT.0.0) IPS(I)=1
       TQPR=TQPR+AL(I+744)*IPS(I)
7        CONTINUE
         TOT = 0.0
       DO 78 I = 745,768
         TOT=TOT + AL(I)
78     CONTINUE
C      INITIALIZATION OF SOME MATRICES USED IN CALCULATIONS

C
       DO 1 I = 1,8
       DO 2 J = 1,5
         IPRAS(I,J) = 0
         LA(J) = 0
         MA(J) = 0
         MTS(J) = 0
         MFTS(J) = 0
2        CONTINUE
         IPR(I) = 0
         ITAR(I) = 0
         QP(I) = 0.0
         DI(I) = 0.0
1        CONTINUE
C
C      FOR THE PARTS SELECTED IN THIS BATCH, CALCULATE # OF TOOLS

C      USED ON EACH MACHINE.
C
       DO 30 I = 1,8
       IF(IPS(I).LE.0) GO TO 30
       CALL TLCNT(ISP(I),IEP(I),AL,MTS)
30     CONTINUE
C
C      FINISH COUNTING TOOLS ON EACH MACHINE. NOW TAKE INTO
C      ACCOUNT COMMON TOOLING AND ADJUST FOR THE SAME.

C
       I = 366
```

```
          J = 381
          DO 40 K = 1,5
          IA = IPS(1)*AL(I)
          IB = IPS(2)*AL(I+10)
          IC = IPS(6)*AL(I+70)
          IF(IA.GT.0.AND.IB.GT.0)  LA(K)=1
          IF(IA.GT.0.AND.IC.GT.0)  LA(K)=1
          IF(IB.GT.0.AND.IC.GT.0)  LA(K)=1
          IF(IA.GT.0.AND.IB.GT.0.AND.IC.GT.0)  LA(K)=2
          IA = IPS(3)*AL(J)
          IB = IPS(7)*AL(J+70)
          IC = IPS(8)*AL(J+85)
          IF(IA.GT.0.AND.IB.GT.0)  MA(K)=1
          IF(IA.GT.0.AND.IC.GT.0)  MA(K)=1
          IF(IB.GT.0.AND.IC.GT.0)  MA(K)=1
          IF(IA.GT.0.AND.IB.GT.0.AND.IC.GT.0)  MA(K)=2
          MTS(K) = MTS(K)-LA(K)-MA(K)
            I = I+1
            J = J+1
   40     CONTINUE
   C
   C      FINISH ACCOUNTING FOR COMMON TOOLING.
   C      NOW OPERATIONS THAT HAVE COMMON TOOLING BUT NOT BEING
   C      PRODUCED ARE ASSIGNED TO INCREASE ROUTING FLEXIBILITY IF
   C      THAT MACHINE IS CAPABLE.
   C
   C      FOR JOBS 1, 2, AND 6
            J = 366
            DO 50 K = 1,5
       IF(AL(J)*IPS(1)+AL(J+10)*IPS(2)+AL(J+70)*IPS(6).EQ.0.0)  GO TO 47
   C       IF(AL(J)+AL(J+10)+AL(J+70).EQ.0.0)  GO TO 47
          IF(PT(2,K).LE.30.)AL(J)  = 1.5*IPS(1)
          IF(PT(4,K).LE.30.)AL(J+10)  = 1.5*IPS(2)
          IF(PT(16,K).LE.30.)  AL(J+70) = 1.5*IPS(6)
   47     J=J+1
   50     CONTINUE
   C
   C      REPEATING THE SAME FOR PARTS 3,7, AND 8
            J = 381
            DO 55 K = 1,5
       IF(AL(J)*IPS(3)+AL(J+70)*IPS(7)+AL(J+85)*IPS(8).EQ.0.0)  GO TO 57
   C       IF(AL(J)+AL(J+70)+AL(J+85).EQ.0.0)  GO TO 57
          IF(PT(5,K).LE.30.)AL(J)  = 1.5*IPS(3)
          IF(PT(19,K).LE.30.)  AL(J+70) = 1.5*IPS(7)
          IF(PT(22,K).LE.30.)  AL(J+85) = 1.5*IPS(8)
   57     J=J+1
   55     CONTINUE
   C
```

```
C       FINISH UPDATING AL(.) MATRIX FOR COMMON TOOLING.

C
C       CALCULATE PRODUCTION ROUTES TO BE USED LATER.

C
            DO 60 I = 1,8
        IF(IPS(I).EQ.0) GO TO 60
        CALL PRDRTS(I,IPR)
  60    CONTINUE
C
C       FINISH CALCULATING PRODUCTION ROUTES.
C
C       COUNTING TOTAL # OF OPERATIONS IN THIS BATCH.
        ITOTOPN = 0
        DO 65 I = 1,8
        ITOTOPN = ITOTOPN+NOFOP(I)*IPS(I)
  65    CONTINUE
C
C       CALCULATE TOTAL FREE SLOTS TO BE ASSIGNED LATER.

            MFSLTS = 0
        DO 100 K = 1,5
            MFTS(K) =100- MTS(K)
            MFSLTS = MFSLTS+MFTS(K)
 100    CONTINUE
C
        WRITE(*,133)(500-MFSLTS)
 133    FORMAT(5X,'TOTAL  TOOLS USED IN PRODUCTION  ARE = ',2X,I3)

        WRITE(*,*)
        WRITE(*,*)
C
C       FOR THE PARTS SELECTED IN THIS BATCH, COUNT SINGLE
C       ASSIGNMENTS
            ITSA = 0
            DO 110 I = 1,8
                IF(IPS(I).LE.0) GO TO 110
            DO 110 J = 1,NOFOP(I)
        IF(IPRAS(I,J).NE.1) GO TO 110
        ITSA = ITSA+1*IPS(I)
 110    CONTINUE
C
C       DEPENDING ON TOTAL FREE SLOTS AND TOTAL SINGLE
C       ASSIGNEMTS WE GO TO SUBROUTINES LEVEL 1 FOR ITSA<=MFSLTS
C       OR TO LEVEL 2 IF MFSLTS < ITSA.
C
C
```

```
       IF(ITSA.GT.MFSLTS) GO TO 786
       IF(ITSA.LE.MFSLTS) CALL LEVEL1(IPS)
       CALL LEVEL1(IPS)

       IF(MFSLTS.EQ.0) GO TO 120
       END IF
C
C      THE LEFT OVER TOOL SLOTS AFTER LEVEL1 ARE NOW ASSIGNED
C      WITH WEIGHTS CALCULATED AS RATIO OF ITS QUANTITY
C      PRODUCED TO TQPR
C
 786      DO 200 I = 1,8
          QP(I) = AL(744+I)
          DI(I) = I
 200   CONTINUE
C
C      ARRANGE QTY PRODUCED IN DESCENDING ORDER
          I = 1
 235      J = I+1
 240   IF(QP(I).GE.QP(J)) GO TO 250
          KOPY=QP(I)
          KOP=DI(I)
          QP(I)=QP(J)
          DI(I)=DI(J)
          QP(J)=KOPY
          DI(J)=KOP
 250   J=J+1
       IF(J.LE.8) GO TO 240
       I=I+1
       IF(I.LE.7) GO TO 235
C
C      FINISH ARRANGING IN A DESCENDING ORDER
C
          LFSLTS=MFSLTS
          DO 705 I = 1,8
       IF(IPS(DI(I)).EQ.0) GO TO 705
       IF(LFSLTS.LE.0) GO TO 705
       N = NINT(LFSLTS*QP(I)*IPS(DI(I))/TQPR)
          IF(N.LT.1) N=1
             ITS(DI(I)) = MIN(LFSLTS,N)
             LFSLTS = LFSLTS - ITS(DI(I))
 705   CONTINUE
C

C      FINISH DISTRIBUTING FREE TOOL SLOTS BASED ON QTY
C      PRODUCED.
C
          ICOUNT = 0
```

```
490     CALL LEVEL2(IPS,ITS)


        IF(MFSLTS.EQ.0) GO TO 120
        IF(ICOUNT.GE.25)GO TO 120
C
C       THE LEFT-OVER TOOLS WILL NOW BE ASSIGNED TO PARTS BASED
C       ON # OF OPERATIONS.  THIS IS TO ASSIGN IF POSSIBLE ALL SLOTS.

C
        DO 300 I = 1,8
          QP(I) = NOFOP(I)
          DI(I) = I
300     CONTINUE
C
C       ARRANGE # OF OPERNS. IN DESCENDING ORDER
        I = 1
335       J = I+1
340     IF(QP(I).GE.QP(J)) GO TO 350
          KOPY=QP(I)
          KOP=DI(I)
          QP(I)=QP(J)
          DI(I)=DI(J)
          QP(J)=KOPY
          DI(J)=KOP
350     J=J+1
        IF(J.LE.8) GO TO 340
        I=I+1
        IF(I.LE.7) GO TO 335
C
C       FINISH ARRANGING IN A DESCENDING ORDER
C
        LFSLTS=MFSLTS
        DO 405 I = 1,8
        IF(IPS(I).EQ.0) GO TO 405
        IF(LFSLTS.LE.0) GO TO 405
      N = NINT(LFSLTS*QP(I)*IPS(DI(I))/ITOTOPN)
        IF(N.LT.1) N=1
          ITS(DI(I)) = MIN(LFSLTS,N)
          LFSLTS = LFSLTS - ITS(DI(I))
405     CONTINUE
        ICOUNT = ICOUNT+1
        GO TO 490
C
C       NOW AGAIN UPDATE AL(.) MATRIX TO TAKE INTO ACCOUNT
C       COMMON TOOLS TO COMPUTE FLEXIBILITY.

C
```

```
C       FOR JOBS 1, 2, AND 6
120         J = 366
            DO 52 K = 1,5
       IF(AL(J)*IPS(1)+AL(J+10)*IPS(2)+AL(J+70)*IPS(6).EQ.0.0)  GO TO 59
         IF(PT(2,K).LE.30.)AL(J)  = 1.5*IPS(1)
         IF(PT(4,K).LE.30.)AL(J+10) = 1.5*IPS(2)
         IF(PT(16,K).LE.30.)  AL(J+70) = 1.5*IPS(6)
59      J=J+1
52      CONTINUE
C
C       REPEATING THE SAME FOR PARTS 3,7, AND 8
            J = 381
            DO 53 K = 1,5
       IF(AL(J)*IPS(3)+AL(J+70)*IPS(7)+AL(J+85)*IPS(8).EQ.0.0)  GO TO 54
         IF(PT(5,K).LE.30.)AL(J)  = 1.5*IPS(3)
         IF(PT(19,K).LE.30.)  AL(J+70) = 1.5*IPS(7)
         IF(PT(22,K).LE.30.)  AL(J+85) = 1.5*IPS(8)
54      J=J+1
53      CONTINUE
C
C       FINISH UPDATING AL(.) MATRIX FOR COMMON TOOLING.


C
C       CALCULATE TOTAL AVAILABLE ROUTES
C
        DO 150 I = 1,8
        IF(IPS(I).LE.0) GO TO 150
        CALL PRDRTS(I,ITAR)
        WRITE(*,135) I,IPR(I),ITAR(I)
135     FORMAT(5X,'PART',I2,5X,'PROD.ROUTES',I5,10X,'TOTAL   ROUTES',I5)
150     CONTINUE
        WRITE(*,*)
        WRITE(*,*)
        WRITE(*,160) ITOTOPN
        WRITE(*,*)
        WRITE(*,161) TQPR
160     FORMAT(5X,'TOTAL # OF OPERATIONS IN THIS BATCH = ',I3)
161     FORMAT(5X,'TOTAL  QUANTITY OF PARTS PRODUCED = ',F10.5)

        WRITE(*,*)
        WRITE(*,*)
        WRITE(*,162)
162     FORMAT(9X,'RF FROM PR. RTS',5X,'RF FROM ALL RTS',
     1  5X,'RF BASED ON 1-(PR/AR)')
        WRITE(*,*)
            PRF = 0.0
            TRF = 0.0
            OTRF=0.0
```

```
        DO 140 I = 1,8
        IF(IPS(I).LE.0)  GO TO 140
          RF1=1.0/IPR(I)
          RF2=1.0/ITAR(I)
         RF3=(1.0*IPR(I))/ITAR(I)
          RF1=1.0-RF1
          RF2=1.0-RF2
          RF3=1.0-RF3
        PRF=PRF+AL(I+744)*RF1/TQPR
        TRF=TRF+AL(I+744)*RF2/TQPR
        OTRF=OTRF+AL(I+744)*RF3/TQPR
        WRITE(*,165)I,RF1,RF2,RF3
165     FORMAT(1X,'PART',2X,I2,4X,F10.5,5X,F10.5,12X,F10.5)
140     CONTINUE
        WRITE(*,*)
        WRITE(*,*)
        WRITE(*,167)(PRF*TQPR/TOT)
        WRITE(*,168)(TRF*TQPR/TOT)

167     FORMAT(5X,'RF FOR THIS BATCH BASED ON PROD. RTS.',F10.5)

168     FORMAT(5X,'RF FOR THIS BATCH BASED ON AVLB. RTS.',F10.5)

        WRITE(*,*)

        WRITE(*,*)
        DO 180 K = 1,5
        WRITE(*,169)K,MFTS(K)
169     FORMAT(5X,'FREE TOOL SLOTS ON MACHINE',2X,I2,2X,'=',2X,I3)

180     CONTINUE
        WRITE(*,*)
        WRITE(*,172)MFSLTS
172     FORMAT(5X,'TOTAL FREE SLOTS REMAINING = ',I3)
        CLOSE(UNIT=8, STATUS = 'KEEP')
        STOP
        END
C
C
C
C       ************************************
C                 SUBROUTINES
C       ************************************
C
C
C       ****************************************************************
C         SUBROUTINE TLCNT.
C         THIS SUBROUTINE CALCULATES NUMBER OF TOOLS USED IN
```

```
C        PRODUCTION ON EACH MACHINE.
C        ************************************************************
C
         SUBROUTINE TLCNT(JJ,JJJ,AL,MTS)
         DIMENSION MTS(5),AL(811)
             DO 20 K = 1,5
             DO 40 J = JJ,JJJ,5
         IF(AL(J).LE.0.0) GO TO 40
             MTS(K)=MTS(K)+1
40           CONTINUE
             JJ=JJ+1
             JJJ=JJJ+1
20           CONTINUE
             RETURN
         END
C
C
C        ************************************************************
C        SUBROUTINE PRDRTS.
C        THIS SUBROUTINES CALCULATES FOR EACH PART CHOSEN
C        IN THE BATCH NUMBER OF ROUTES USED IN PRODUCTION
C        (ALSO INCLUDES ROUTES AVAILABLE SINCE THERE IS A
C        COMMON TOOL PRESENT ON THE MACHINE.
C        ************************************************************
C
         SUBROUTINE PRDRTS(I,MP)
         COMMON AL(811),PT(24,5),MFTS(5),IPRAS(8,5),MFSLTS
         DIMENSION MP(8),ISP(8),IEP(8)
         DATA(ISP(I),I=1,8)/361,376,381,391,406,426,451,461/
         DATA(IEP(I),I=1,8)/371,376,386,401,421,446,456,476/
             JJ=ISP(I)
             JJJ=IEP(I)
             L = 1
           MP(I) = 1
             DO 90 J = JJ,JJJ,5
               IP=0
               M=J
             DO 80 K = 1,5
         IF(AL(M).LE.0.0) GO TO 85
C        IF(I.EQ.5) WRITE(*,*)AL(M)
             IP=IP+1
85           M=M+1
80           CONTINUE
             IPRAS(I,L) = IP
             MP(I)=MP(I)*IP
             L=L+1
```

```
90      CONTINUE
        RETURN
      END
C
C     ************************************************************
C        SUBROUTINE LEVEL1.
C        THIS SUBROUTINE ASSIGNS FIRST AN ALTERNATE M/C
C        FOR SINGLE ASSIGNEMNTS.  BEFORE DOING THIS, A
C        TROUBLE COUNTER INDICATING OPN. VS. M/C COMBIN.
C        INFEASIBLE FOR EACH PART IS COMPUTED.  A PART
C        WITH HIGHEST TC IS FIRST CHOSEN AND PROVIDED
C        WITH ALT. M/C.  THIS REDUCES THE RISK OF NOT
C        ABLE TO ASSIGNING AN OPN. WITH ALT. ASSIGNMNT.
C
C     ************************************************************
C
      SUBROUTINE LEVEL1(IPS)
      COMMON AL(811),PT(24,5),MFTS(5),IPRAS(8,5),MFSLTS
      DIMENSION IND(8),NOFOP(8)
      DIMENSION ITC(8),IPS(8),QP(8),DI(8)
      DATA(IND(I),I=1,8)/1,4,5,7,10,14,19,21/
      DATA(NOFOP(I),I=1,8)/3,1,2,3,4,5,2,4/
C     FOR EACH JOB IN THIS BATCH, GET # OF MACHINES ON WHICH
C     THEIR SINGLE ASSIGNMENTS CANNOT BE DONE. TROUBLE
C     COUNTER.
C
      DO 300 I = 1,8
      IF(IPS(I).EQ.0) GO TO 300
        ITC(I)=0
      DO 310 J = 1,NOFOP(I)
      IF(IPRAS(I,J).NE.1) GO TO 310
        DO 320 K = 1,5
      IF(MFTS(K).EQ.0) GO TO 320
      IF(PT(IND(I)+J-1,K).GT.30.0) THEN
        ITC(I) = ITC(I)+1
      END IF
320       CONTINUE
310       CONTINUE
300       CONTINUE
C
C     NOW THAT JOB WITH HIGHEST INFEASIBLE MACHINE
C     ASSIGNMENTS IS GIVEN TOP PRIORITY AND ITS SINGLE
C     ASSIGNMENTS ARE NOW PROVIDED WITH ALTERNATE MACHINES.
C
      DO 200 KK = 1,8
        QP(KK)=ITC(KK)
        DI(KK) = KK
200       CONTINUE
```

```
             K = 1
235          J = K+1
240    IF(QP(K).GE.QP(J)) GO TO 250
             KOPY=QP(K)
             KOP=DI(K)
             QP(K)=QP(J)
             DI(K)=DI(J)
             QP(J)=KOPY
             DI(J)=KOP
250    J=J+1
       IF(J.LE.8) GO TO 240
       K=K+1
       IF(K.LE.7) GO TO 235
C
C      FINISH ARRANGING IN A DESCENDING ORDER
             DO 400 I = 1,8
       IF(IPS(DI(I)).EQ.0) GO TO 400
             M = DI(I)
          DO 530 L = 1,NOFOP(M)
       IF(IPRAS(M,L).NE.1) GO TO 530
             IFLAG = 0
             NM=0
          DO 542 K = 1,5
       IF(IFLAG.EQ.1) GO TO 542
       IF(MFTS(K).EQ.0) GO TO 540
       IF(PT(IND(M)+L-1,K).GT.30.0) GO TO 540
          LL = 1+5*(IND(M)-IND(1)+L-1)+360+NM
       IF(AL(LL).GT.0.0) GO TO 540
          AL(LL) = 1.5
          IPRAS(M,L) = IPRAS(M,L)+1
          MFTS(K) = MFTS(K)-1
            MFSLTS=MFSLTS-1
            IFLAG = 1
540    NM=NM+1
542    CONTINUE
530    CONTINUE
400    CONTINUE
             RETURN
       END
C
C      ************************************************************
C      SUBROUTINE LEVEL2.
C      THIS SUBROUTINE WILL FIRST FIND THAT JOB THAT HAS
C      OPN. VS. M/C INFEASIBILITY LIKE BEFORE. THE ONE
C      WITH HIGHEST # IS CHOSEN. THEN ITS OPNS. ARE
C      ARRANGED IN ASCENDING ORDER TO GET THAT OPN.
C      THAT HAS LEAST # OF ASSIGNMENTS AND THEN A
C      M/C TO THAT SINCE THIS MAXIMIZES RF. THIS
```

```
C          REARRANGEMENT  IS DONE # OF TIMES EQUAL TO HOW
C          MANY SLOTS ARE GIVEN TO THIS PART.
C          *************************************************************
C
      SUBROUTINE  LEVEL2(IPS,ITS)
      COMMON AL(811),PT(24,5),MFTS(5),IPRAS(8,5),MFSLTS
      DIMENSION  IND(8),NOFOP(8)
      DIMENSION  ITC(8),ITS(8),LL(5),KL(5),IPS(8),QP(8),DI(8)
      DATA(IND(I),I=1,8)/1,4,5,7,10,14,19,21/
      DATA(NOFOP(I),I=1,8)/3,1,2,3,4,5,2,4/
C     DATA(IPS(I),I=1,8)/1,1,1,1,1,0,0,0/
C
C
C     GET THAT JOB THAT HAS HIGHER RISK.
C
          DO 710 I = 1,8
            ITC(I)=0
      IF(IPS(I).EQ.0)  GO TO 710
      IF(ITS(I).EQ.0)  GO TO 710
C          WRITE(*,*)ITS(I),I
          DO 715 J = 1,NOFOP(I)
          DO 720 K = 1,5
      IF(MFTS(K).EQ.0)  GO TO 720
      IF(PT(IND(I)+J-1,K).GT.30.0)  THEN
            ITC(I)=ITC(I)+1
          END IF
720   CONTINUE
715   CONTINUE
710   CONTINUE
          DO 200 KK = 1,8
            QP(KK)=ITC(KK)
            DI(KK) = KK
200       CONTINUE
            K = 1
235         J = K+1
240   IF(QP(K).GE.QP(J)) GO TO 250
            KOPY=QP(K)
            KOP=DI(K)
            QP(K)=QP(J)
            DI(K)=DI(J)
            QP(J)=KOPY
            DI(J)=KOP
250   J=J+1
      IF(J.LE.8) GO TO 240
      K=K+1
      IF(K.LE.7) GO TO 235
C
C     FINISH ARRANGING IN A DESCENDING ORDER
          DO 800 I = 1,8
```

```
      IF(IPS(DI(I)).EQ.0) GO TO 800
      IF(ITS(DI(I)).EQ.0) GO TO 800
        MM=DI(I)
      IF(ITS(MM).LE.0) GO TO 800
C         WRITE(*,*)ITS(MM),MM
          DO 820 M = 1,ITS(MM)
          DO 830 L = 1,NOFOP(MM)
            LL(L) = L
            KL(L) = IPRAS(MM,L)
 830      CONTINUE
C
C     ARRANGE THE OPN. ASSGNMNT. IN ASCENDING ORDERSO THAT A
C     FREE SLOT IS ASSIGNED TO THE LOWEST ONE TO MAX RF.

C
            K = 1
 835        J=K+1
 840   IF(KL(K).GE.KL(J)) GO TO 850
            KOPY = KL(K)
            KOP = LL(K)
            KL(K)=KL(J)
            LL(K)=LL(J)
            KL(J)=KOPY
            LL(J)=KOP
 850   J=J+1

      IF(J.LE.NOFOP(MM)) GO TO 840
            K = K+1
      IF(K.LE.NOFOP(MM)-1) GO TO 835
C
C     FINISH ARRANGING.
C
            IFLAG = 0
         DO 860 L = NOFOP(MM),1,-1
C        DO 860 L = 1,NOFOP(MM)
      IF(IFLAG.EQ.1) GO TO 860
      IF(IPRAS(MM,LL(L)).GE.5) GO TO 860
        NM=0
        DO 872 K =1,5
      IF(IFLAG.EQ.1) GO TO 872
      IF(MFTS(K).LE.0) GO TO 870
      IF(PT(IND(MM)+LL(L)-1,K).GE.30.0) GO TO 870
      LML = 1+5*(IND(MM)-IND(1)+LL(L)-1)+360+NM
      IF(AL(LML).GT.0.0) GO TO 870
        AL(LML) = 1.5
        IPRAS(MM,LL(L)) = IPRAS(MM,LL(L))+1
        MFTS(K) = MFTS(K)-1
        MFSLTS=MFSLTS-1
```

```
          IFLAG = 1
870    NM=NM+1
872    CONTINUE
860    CONTINUE
820    CONTINUE
800    CONTINUE
          RETURN
       END
C
C
       SUBROUTINE  LRMREAD(AL)
       DIMENSION  AL(811)
C
       OPEN(UNIT = 9, FILE = '/FFUMMX10 SOL',STATUS='OLD')
       READ(9,2)
2      FORMAT(72X)
9      FORMAT(24X,F10.5,38X)
       READ(9,9)(AL(I),I=1,49)
       II= 50
       III=100
11     READ(9,2)
       READ(9,2)
       IF (III.GE.811) III=811
       DO 7 I=II,III
       READ(9,9)AL(I)
7      CONTINUE
       IF(III.EQ.811) GO TO 15
       II = II+51
       III=III+51
       GO TO 11
15     CLOSE(UNIT=9, STATUS='KEEP')
       RETURN
        END
```

A Typical Output

TOTAL TOOLS USED IN PRODUCTION ARE =   16

PART 1	PROD.ROUTES	24	TOTAL ROUTES	80
PART 2	PROD.ROUTES	4	TOTAL ROUTES	5
PART 4	PROD.ROUTES	2	TOTAL ROUTES	18
PART 7	PROD.ROUTES	2	TOTAL ROUTES	9

TOTAL # OF OPERATIONS IN THIS BATCH = 9

TOTAL QUANTITY OF PARTS PRODUCED =   78.00000

                RF FROM PR. RTS   RF FROM ALL RTS

PART   1   0.95833   0.98750
PART   2   0.75000   0.80000
PART   4   0.50000   0.94444
PART   7   0.50000   0.88889

        RF FOR THIS BATCH BASED ON PROD. RTS.   0.73771
        RF FOR THIS BATCH BASED ON AVLB. RTS.   0.91017

        FREE TOOL SLOTS ON MACHINE   1 =   0
        FREE TOOL SLOTS ON MACHINE   2 =   0
        FREE TOOL SLOTS ON MACHINE   3 =   0
        FREE TOOL SLOTS ON MACHINE   4 =   0
        FREE TOOL SLOTS ON MACHINE   5 =   0

        TOTAL FREE SLOTS REMAINING = 0

References

Afentakis, P., "An Optimal Scheduling Strategy for Flexible Manufacturing Systems," Working Paper # 85-D12, Dept. of Industrial Engineering and Operations Research, Syracuse University, 1985.

Afentakis, P., "Maximum Throughput in Flexible Manufacturing Systems," *Proceedings of the 2nd ORSA/TIMS Conference on Flexible Manufacturing Systems,* pp. 509-520, 1986.

Akella, R., Choong, Y.F., and Gershwin, S.B., "Performance of Hierarchical Production Scheduling Policy," *IEEE Transactions, Components Hybrids Manufacturing Technology,* CHMT-7, pp. 225-240, 1984.

Akella, R., Choong, Y.F., and Gershwin, S.B., "Real Time Production Scheduling of an Automated Card Line," *Annals of Operations Research,* 3, pp. 403-425, 1985.

Ammons, J.C., Lofgren, C.B., and McGinnis, L.F., "A Large Scale Workstation Loading Problem," *Annals of Operations Research,* 3, pp. 319-332, 1985.

Ayers, R.U., Haywood, W., Merchant, M.E., Ranta, J., and Warnecke, H.-J., (Eds.,) *Computer Integrated Manufacturing,* Volume II, Chapman & Hall, New York, 1992.

Barash, M.M., "Speculation on the Future of Numerical Controls," paper no. 78-WA/DSC-9, presented at the American Society of Manufacturing Engineers Conference, San Francisco, December, 1978.

Bastos, J.M., "Batching and Routing: Two Functions in the Operational Planning of Flexible Manufacturing Systems," *European Journal of Operations Research,* 33, pp. 230-244, 1987.

Bernardo J.J., and Mohamed, Z.M., "The Measurement and Use of Operational Flexibility in the Loading of Flexible Manufacturing Systems", *European Journal of Operations Research,* 60, pp. 144-155, 1992.

Bernardo, J.J., and Mohamed, Z.M., "The Effect of Stochastic Demand on Minimum Cost Loading Policy for an FMS," presented at the Annual Decision Science Meeting, Las Vegas, 1988(a).

Bernardo, J.J., and Mohamed, Z.M., "Effect of Demand Variability on Inventory and Machine Loading in a Flexible Manufacturing System," *Symposium on Advanced Manufacturing,* Lexington, Kentucky, pp. 73-78, 1988b.

Berrada Mohammed, and Stecke, K.E., "A Branch and Bound Approach for Machine Loading in Flexible Manufacturing Systems," *Management Science,* 32, # 10, pp. 1316-1335, 1986.

Bitran, G.R., Haas, E.A., and Hax, A.C., "Hierarchical Production Planning: A Single Stage System," *Operations Research,* 29, no. 4, pp. 717-743, 1981.

Bitran, G.R, Haas, E.A., and Hax, A.C., "Hierarchical Production Planning: A Two Stage System," *Operations Research,* 30, no. 2, pp. 232-251, 1982.

Bitran, G.R., and Tirupati, D., "Trade-off Curves, Targeting and Balancing in Manufacturing Networks", Working paper, The University of Texas at Austin, 1987.

Brill, D., and Mandelbaum, M., "Measures of Flexibility for Production Systems", *Proceedings of the IXth International Conference on Production Research,* pp. 2474-2481, 1987.

Brill, D., and Mandelbaum, M., "On Measures of Flexibility in Manufacturing Systems", *International Journal of Production Research,* 27, pp. 747-756, 1989.

Brill, D. and Mandelbaum, M., "Measurement of Adaptivity and Flexibility in Production Systems", *European Journal of Operational Research,* 49, pp. 325-332, 1990.

Browne, J., Dubois, D., Rathmil, K., Sethi, S.P., and Stecke, K.E., "Classification of Flexible Manufacturing Systems," *FMS Magazine,* 2(2), pp. 114-117, 1984.

Buzacott, J.A., "Optimal Operating Rules for Automated Manufacturing Systems," *IEEE Transactions on Automatic Control,* February, 1982a.

Buzacott, J.A., "The Fundamental Principles of Flexibility in Manufacturing Systems," *Proceedings of 1st International Conference on Flexible Manufacturing Systems,* pp. 13-22, 1982.

Buzacott, J.A., and Shanthikumar, J.G., " Models for understanding Flexible Manufacturing Systems," *AIIE Transactions,* 12, #4, pp. 339-349, 1980.

Buzacott, J.A., and Yao, D.D., "On Queuing Network Models of Flexible Manufacturing Systems", *Queuing Systems Theory and Applications,* 1, pp. 5-27, 1986.

Caie, J., Linden, J., and Maxwell, W.L.," Solution of a Machine Load Planning Problem," Technical report # 396, School of Operations Research & Industrial Engineering, Cornell University, Ithaca, New York, 1978.

Carter, M.F., "Designing Flexibility into Automated Manufacturing Systems," *Proceedings of the Second ORSA/TIMS Conference on Flexible Manufacturing Systems: Operations Research Models and Applications,* Stecke, K.E. and Suri, R., (editors), 1986.

Cavaille, J.B., and Dubois, D., "Heuristics Methods Based on Mean Value Analysis for Flexible Manufacturing System Performance Evaluation," *Proceedings of the 21st. IEEE Conference on Decision and Control,* Orlando, Florida, pp. 1061-1065, 1982.

Chakravarty, A.K., and Shtub, A., " Selecting Parts and Loading Flexible Manufacturing Systems," *Proceedings of 1st. ORSA/TIMS Special Conference on FMS's,* pp. 284-   ,1984.

Chang, Y.L., and Sullivan, R.S., "Real Time Scheduling of FMS," TIMS/ORSA, San Francisco, May 1984.

Chang, Y.L., Sullivan, R.S., and Bagchi, U., "Experimental Investigation of Real Time Scheduling in Flexible Manufacturing Systems," *Annals of Operations Research,* 3, pp. 355-377, 1985.

Chang, T.C., Wysk, R.A., and Wang, H.P., *Computer Aided Manufacturing,* Prentice Hall, 1991.

Chatterjee, A., Cohen, A.M., and Maxwell, W.J., "Manufacturing Flexibility: Models and Measurements," *Proceedings of the First ORSA/TIMS Special Interest Conference on Flexible Manufacturing Systems,* 1984.

Chen, I.J., "Interfacing the Loading and Routing Decisions for Flexibility and Productivity of Flexible Manufacturing Systems," Ph.D. Dissertation, University of Kentucky, 1989.

Chung, C.H., " A Maximal Covering Model for Loading Flexible Manufacturing Systems," *Proceedings of the First Symposium on Real Time Optimization in Automated Manufacturing Facilities,* Washington D.C., January, pp. 213-223, 1986a.

Chung, C.H., " Loading Flexible Manufacturing Systems: A Heuristic Approach," *Computers and Industrial Engineering,* 11, # 1-4, pp. 246-250, 1986b.

Chung, C.H., and Chen, I.J., "Managing the Flexibility of Flexible Manufacturing Systems for Competitive Edge," in M.S. Liberatore (Ed.) *Selection and Evaluation of Advanced Manufacturing Technologies,* Berlin, Springer-Verlag, pp. 281-305, 1990.

Cox, T. Jr., "Toward the Measurement of Manufacturing Flexibility," *Production and Inventory Management Journal,* First Quarter, pp. 68-72, 1989.

Dallery, Y., and Frein, Y., "An Efficient Method to Determine the Optimal Configuration of a Flexible Manufacturing System," *Proceedings of the 2nd. ORSA/TIMS Special Conference on FMS,* pp. 269-281, 1986.

Draper Labs, *Flexible Manufacturing Systems,* 1984.

Dubois, D., and Stecke, K.E., "Using Petrinets to Represent Production Processes," *Proceedings of the 22nd. Conference on Decision and Control,* San Antonio, Texas, 1983.

Dupont-Gatelmand, K., "A Survey of Flexible Manufacturing Systems," *Journal of Manufacturing Systems,* 1, # 1, 1982.

Edghill, J.S., and Creswell, C., "FMS Control Strategy - A Survey of the Determining Characteristics," *Proceedings of the fourth International Conference on Flexible manufacturing Systems,* pp. 305-315, 1985.

El Maraghy, H.A., "Simulation and Graphical animation of Advanced Manufacturing Systems," *Journal of Manufacturing Systems,* 1, # 1, pp. 53-63, 1982.

Erschler, J., Levegne, D., and Roubellat, F., "Periodic Loading of Flexible Manufacturing Systems," *Advances in Production Management Systems,* pp. 401-413, 1984.

Erschler, J., Roubellat, F., and Thuriot, C., "Steady State Scheduling of a Flexible Manufacturing System with Periodic Releasing and Flow Time Constraints," *Annals of Operations Research,* 3, pp. 333-353, 1985.

Gershwin, S.B., Akella, R., and Choong, Y.F., "Short-term Production Planning of an Automated Manufacturing Facility," *IBM Journal of Research Development,* 9, pp. 392-400, 1985.

Gerwin, D., "Do's and Dont's of Computerized Manufacturing," *Harvard Business Review,* 60, no. 2, pp. 107-116, 1982.

Gerwin, D. "Manufacturing Flexibility: A Strategic Perspective", *Management Science,* 39/4, pp. 395-410, 1993.

Graham, M.B.W., and Rosenthal, S.R., "Institutional Aspects of Process Procurement for Flexible Machining Systems", Boston University, School of Management, Boston, MA, 1986.

Greene, T.J., and Sadowski, R.P., "A Mixed Integer program for Loading and Scheduling Multiple Flexible Manufacturing Cells," *European Journal of Operations Research,* 24, pp. 379-386, 1986.

Gupta, D., and Buzacott, J.A., "A Framework for Understanding Flexibility of Manufacturing Systems," *Journal of Manufacturing Systems,* 8, no. 2, pp. 89-97, 1989.

Gupta, Y.P., and Goyal, S., "Flexibility of Manufacturing Systems: Concepts and Measurements," *European Journal of Operations Research,* 43, pp. 119-135, 1989.

Gustavsson, S.V., "Flexibility and Productivity in Complex Production Processes," *International Journal of Production Research,* 22, no. 5, pp. 801-808, 1984.

Hahne, E., "Dynamic Routing in Unreliable Manufacturing Network With Limited Resources," M.I.T. Laboratory for Information and Decision Systems, Report No. LIDS-TH-1063, 1981.

Hildebrant, R.R., "Scheduling Flexible Manufacturing Systems When Machines are Prone to Failure," Ph.D. Dissertation, Dept. of aeronautics and Astronautics, MIT, cambridge, Massachusetts, 1980.

Hildebrant, R.R., "Scheduling Flexible Manufacturing Systems Using Mean Value Analysis," *IEEE Conference on Decision and Control,* pp. 701-706, 1980.

Hildebrant, R.R., and Suri, R., "Methodology and Multi-level Algorithm Structure for Scheduling and Real Time Control of Flexible Manufacturing Systems," *Proceedings of 3 rd International Symposium on Large Engineering Systems,* Memorial University of New Foundland, Canada, July, 1980.

Hitz, K.L., "Scheduling of Flow Shops I," Technical Report 879, LIDS, MIT, 1979.

Hitz, K.L., "Scheduling of Flow Shops II," Technical Report 1049, LIDS, MIT, 1980.

Horowitz, E., and Sahni, S., "Computing Partitions with Application to the Knapsack Problem," *Journal of the Association for Computing Machinery,* 21, #2, pp. 277-292, 1974.

Hung, M.S., and Fisk, J.C., "An Algorithm for 0-1 Multiple Knapsack Problem," *Naval Research Logistics Quarterly,* 25, #3, pp.571-579, 1978.

Hutchinson, G.K., "The Control of Flexible Manufacturing Systems: Required Information and Control Structures," *IFAC Symposium on Information-Control Problems in Manufacturing Technology,* Tokyo, Japan, October 1977.

Hutchinson, G.K., and Hughes, J.J., "A Generalized Model of Flexible Manufacturing Systems," Kearney and Trecker Corp., 1977.

Hutchinson, G.K., and Sinha, D., "A Quantification of the Value of Flexibility," *Journal of Manufacturing Systems,* 8, no. 1, pp. 47-57, 1989.

Hwang, S., "A Constraint Directed Method to Solve Part selection problem in Flexible Manufacturing Systems," *Proceedings of the 2nd. ORSA/TIMS Special Conference on FMS,* pp. 297-309, 1986.

Hwang, S., and Shogun, A.W., "Modeling and Solving an FMS Part Selection Problem," *International Journal of Production Research,* 27, no. 8, pp. 1349-1366, 1989.

Ito, Y., "Evaluation of FMS: State of the Art regarding How to evaluate System Flexibility," *Robotic & Computer Integrated Manufacturing,* 3(3), pp. 327-334, 1987.

Jaikumar, R., "Post Industrial Manufacturing," *Harvard Business Review,* 64(6), pp. 69-76, 1986.

Kimemia, J.G., "Hierarchical Control of Production in Flexible Manufacturing Systems," PhD. Dissertation, Rep. # LIDS-TH-1215, LIDS, MIT, 1982.

Kimemia, J.G., and Gershwin, S.B., "Network Flow optimization in Flexible Manufacturing Systems," *Proceedings of the IEEE Conference on Decision Control,* pp. 633-639, 1979.

Kimemia, J.G., and Gershwin, S.B., "An Algorithm for the Computer Control of a Flexible Manufacturing System," *IIE Transactions,* 15, pp. 353-362, 1983.

Kimemia, J.G., and Gershwin, S.B., "Flow Optimization in Flexible Manufacturing Systems," *International Journal of Production Research,* 23, pp. 81-96, 1985.

King, J.R., "Machine - Component Grouping in Production Flow Analysis: Approach Using a Rank Order Clustering Algorithm," *International Journal of Production Research,* 18, pp. 218- , 1980.

Kiran, A.S., and Tansel, B.C., "The System Set-up in Flexible Manufacturing Systems," *Proceedings of the 2nd ORSA/TIMS Conference on Flexible Manufacturing Systems,* pp. 321-332, 1986.

Kochan, A., "FMS is for the Big Boys in the U.S.", *The FMS Magazine,* July, pp. 134-135, 1985.

Kouvelis, P., "Machine and Planning Problems in Flexible Manufacturing Systems: A Critical Review", Working paper series, Management Department, Graduate School of Business, The University of Texas at Austin, 1989.

Kouvelis, P., and Lee, H.L., "Block Angular Structures and the Loading Problem in Flexible Manufacturing Systems," *Operations Research,* 39, no. 4, pp. 666-676, 1991.

Kumar, K.R., Kusiak, A., and Vanelli, A., "Grouping of Parts and Components in Flexible Manufacturing Systems," *European Journal of Operations Research,* 24, pp. 387-397, 1986.

Kumar, V., "On Measurement of Flexibility in Flexible Manufacturing Systems: An Information-Theoretic Approach," *Proceedings of the Second ORSA/TIMS Conference on Flexible Manufacturing Systems: Operations Research Models and Applications,* Stecke, K.E. and Suri, R., (editors), 1986.

Kumar, V., and Kumar, U., "Five Years into Measuring manufacturing Flexibility," Presented at APORS'88 Meeting, Seoul, Korea, 1988.

Kusiak, A., "Flexible Manufacturing System: A Structural Approach," *International Journal of Production Research,* 23, no. 6, pp. 1057-1073, 1985.

Kusiak, A., "The Part Families Problem in Flexible Manufacturing Systems," *Annals of Operations Research,* 3, pp. 279-300, 1985.

Kusiak, A., "Loading Models in Flexible Manufacturing Systems," a Chapter in *Flexible Manufacturing: Recent Developments in FMS, CAD/CAM, CIM,* Raouf, A., and Ahmad, S.I., (eds.), 1985.

Kusiak, A., "Application of Operational Research Models and techniques in Flexible Manufacturing Systems," *European Journal of Operations Research,* 24, pp. 336-345, 1986.

Lashkari, R.S., Dutta, S.P., and Padhye, A.M., "A new formulation of operation allocation problem in Flexible Manufacturing Systems: Mathematical modelling and computational experience", *International Journal of Production Research,* 25, pp. 1267-1283, 1987.

Maimon, O.Z., and Choong, Y.F., "Dynamic Routing in Re-entrant Flexible Manufacturing Systems," *Robotics and Computer Aided Manufacturing,* 3, pp. 295-300, 1987.

Maimon, O.Z., and Gershwin, S.B., "Dynamic Scheduling and Routing for Flexible Manufacturing Systems that have Unreliable Machines," *Operations Research,* 36, #2, pp. 279-292, 1988.

Mandelbaum, M., "Flexibility in Decision Making: An Exploration and Unification," Ph.D. Thesis, Dept. of Industrial Engineering, University of Toronto, Canada, 1978.

Mayer, R.J., and Talvage, J.J., "Simulation of Computerized Manufacturing Systems," Report # 4, NSF Grant # APR 74-15256, 1976.

Morin, T.L., and Marsten, R.E., "An Algorithm for Nonlinear Knapsack Problems," *Management Science,* 22, # 10, pp. 1147-1158, 1976.

Mortimer, J., (Ed.,), "The FMS Report: Ingersoll Engineers," *IFS Publications,* 1984.

Nof, S.Y., Barash, M.M., and Solberg, J.J., "Operational Control of Item Flow in Versatile Manufacturing Systems," *International Journal of Production Research,* 17, pp. 479, 1979.

Noori, H., *Managing the Dynamics of New Technology,* Prentice Hall, 1990.

O'Grady, P.J., and Menon, U., "A Multiple Criteria Approach for Production Planning of Automated Manufacturing," *Engineering Optimization,* 8, pp. 161-175, 1985.

Olker, R., "Application of the Minicomputer to Control a Large Flexible Manufacturing System," *Understanding Manufacturing Systems* (Kearney and Trecker Co.).

Olsder, G.J., and Suri, R., "Time Optimal Control of Parts from Routing in a manufacturing System with Failure Prone Machines," *Proceedings of 19th IEEE conference on Decision & Control,* Albuquerque, New Mexico, 1980.

Primerose, P.L., and Leonard, R., "Conditions under which Flexible Manufacturing is Financially Viable," *Proceedings of the 3rd. International Conference on Flexible Manufacturing Systems,* 1984.

Rajagopalan, S., "Formulation and Heuristic Solutions for Parts Grouping and Tool Loading in Flexible manufacturing Systems," *Proceedings of the Second ORSA/TIMS Conference on Flexible Manufacturing Systems,* pp. 311-320, 1986.

Ranta, J., "FMS Investment as a Multiobjective Decision-Making Problem", Unpublished Manuscript, International Institute for Applied Systems Analysis, Laxenburg, Austria, 1989.

Rao, M.R., "Cluster Analysis and Mathematical Programming," *Journal of Amer. Statist. Assoc.,* 66, pp. 622-626, 1971.

Reich, R.B., *The Next American Frontier,* Times Books, New York, 1983.

Rinnooy Kan, A.H.G., "Machine Scheduling Problems," Martinus Mijhoff, The Hague, 1976.

Sahni, S., and Harowitz, E., "Combinatorial Problems: Reducibility and Approximation," *Operations Research,* 26, # 5, pp. 718-759, 1978.

Sarin, S.C., and Chen, C.S., "The Machine Loading and Tool Allocation Problem in a Flexible Manufacturing System", *International Journal of Production Research,* 25/7, pp. 1081-1094, 1987.

Sawik, T., "Modeling and Scheduling a Flexible Manufacturing System," *European Journal of Operational Research,* 45, pp.177-190, 1990.

Schriber, T.J., and Stecke, K.E., "Machine Utilizations and Production Rates Achieved by Using Balanced FMS Production Ratios in a Simulated setting," *Proceedings of the 2nd ORSA/TIMS Conference on Flexible Manufacturing Systems,* pp. 405-416, 1986.

Secco-Suardo, G., "Optimization of a Closed Network of Queues," Report # ESL-FR-834-3, Electronic Systems Laboratory, MIT, Cambridge, Massachusetts, 1979.

Seidman, A., and Schweitzer, P.J., "Part Selection Policy for a Flexible manufacturing Cell Feeding Several production Lines," *IIE Transactions,* pp. 355-362, 1984.

Sethi, A.K., and Sethi, S.P., "Flexibility in Manufacturing: A Survey," *International Journal of Flexible Manufacturing Systems,* 2, no. 4, pp. 289-341, 1990.

Shanker, K., and Tzen, Y.J.J., "A loading and Dispatching Problem in a random Flexible Manufacturing Systems," *International Journal of Production Research,* 23, pp. 579-595, 1985.

Shannon, C.E., "A Mathematical Theory of Communication," *Bell Sys. Tech. J,* 27, pp. 379-423, 633-659, 1948.

Shanthikumar, J.G., "On the Superiority of balanced Load in a Flexible Manufacturing Systems," Technical Report, Dept. of Industrial Engineering and Operations Research, Syracuse University, New York, 1982.

Shanthikumar, J.G., and Buzacott, J.A., "On the Approximation of the Single Server Queue," *International Journal of Production Research,* 18, pp. 761-773, 1980.

Shanthikumar, J.G., and Buzacott, J.A., "Open Queuing Network Models of Dynamic Job Shops," *International Journal of Production Research,* 19, pp. 255-266, 1981.

Shanthikumar, J.G., and Sargent, R.G., "A Hybrid Simulation / Analytical Model of a Computerized Manufacturing System," Working Paper 80-017, Dept. of Industrial Engineering and Operations Research, Syracuse University, 1980.

Shanthikumar, J.G., and Stecke, K.E., "Reducing Work in Process Inventory in certain classes of Flexible Manufacturing Systems," *European Journal of Operations Research,* 26, pp. 266-271, 1986.

Slack, N., "Manufacturing Systems Flexibility-An Assessment Procedure", *Computer Integrated Manufacturing Systems,* 1/1, pp. 25-31, 1988.

Smith, M.L., Ramesh, R., Dudek, R.A., and Blair, E.L., "Characteristics of U.S. Flexible Manufacturing Systems - A Survey," *Proceedings of the Second ORSA/TIMS Conference on Flexible Manufacturing Systems,* pp. 477-486, 1986.

Solberg, J.J., "A Mathematical Model of Computerized Manufacturing Systems," *International Conference on Production Research,* Tokyo, Japan, 1977.

Solberg, J.J., "Capacity Planning with a Stochastic Workflow Model," *Journal of the AIIE,* 1983.

Solberg, J.J., and Nof, S.Y., "Analysis of Flow Control in Alternative Manufacturing Configurations," *Journal of Dynamic Systems, Measurement and Control,* 1980.

Son, Y.K., and Park, C.S., "Economic Measure of Productivity, Quality, and Flexibility in Advanced Manufacturing Systems," *Journal of Manufacturing Systems,* 6, no. 3, pp. 193-207, 1987.

Stecke, K.E., "Production planning for Flexible Manufacturing Systems," Ph.D. Dissertation, School of Industrial Engineering, Purdue University, West Lafayette, Indiana, 1981.

Stecke, K.E., "Formulation and Solution of Nonlinear Integer Production Planning Problems for Flexible Manufacturing Systems," *Management Science,* 29, no. 3, pp. 273-288, 1983a.

Stecke, K.E., "A Hierarchical Approach to Solving Machine Grouping and Loading Problems of Flexible Manufacturing Systems," *European Journal of Operations Research,* 24, pp. 369-378, 1986.

Stecke, K.E., and Kim, I., "A Study of FMS Part type Selection Approaches for Short-term Production Planning," Working Paper # 498-b, Division of Research, Graduate school of Business administration, The University of Michigan, 1987.

Stecke, K.E., and Morin, T.L., "The optimality of Balancing Workloads in Certain Types of Flexible Manufacturing Systems," *European Journal of Operations Research,* 20, pp. 68-82, 1985.

Stecke, K.E., and Solberg, J.J., "The CMS Loading Problem," Report # 20, NSF Grant # APR 74 15256, School of Industrial Engineering, Purdue university, West lafayette, Indiana, February, 1981a.

Stecke, K.E., and Solberg, J.J., "Loading and Control Policies for a Flexible Manufacturing System," *International Journal of Production Research,* 19, no. 5, pp. 481-490, 1981b.

Stecke, K.E., and Solberg, J.J., "The Optimality of Unbalancing Both Work-loads and Machine Group Sizes in Closed Queuing Networks of Multiple Server Queues," *Operations Research,* 33, pp. 882-910, 1985.

Stecke, K.E., and Talbot, F.B., "Heuristics for Loading Flexible Manufacturing Systems," a Chapter in *Flexible Manufacturing: Recent Developments in FMS, CAD/CAM, CIM,* Raouf, A., and Ahmad, S.I., (eds.), pp. 73-85, 1985.

Suarez, F., and Michael, A.C., and Charles, H.F., "Flexibility and Performance: A Literature Critique and Strategic Framework", Sloan School, MIT, Cambridge, MA, 1991.

Suri, R., "New Techniques for Modelling and Control of Flexible Automated Manufacturing Systems," *Proceedings of the 1981 IFAC,* Kyoto, Japan, 1981.

Suri, R., "Robustness of Queuing Network Formulae," *Journal of the ACM,* 1983.

Suri, R., and Hildebrant, R.R., "Modeling Flexible Manufacturing systems Using Mean Value Analysis," *Journal of Manufacturing Systems,* 3(1), pp. 27-38, 1984.

Suri, R., and Whitney, C.K., "Decision Support Requirements in Flexible Manufacturing Systems," *Journal of Manufacturing Systems,* 1, pp. 61-69, 1984.

Swamidass, P.M., *Manufacturing Flexibility,* Monograph No. 2, Operations Management Assoc., January, 1988.

Townsend, W., "Minimizing the Maximum Penalty in the Two Machine Shop," *Management Science,* 24, # 2, pp. 230-234, 1977.

Tsitsiklis, J.N., "Optimal Dynamic Routing in an Unreliable Manufacturing System," M.I.T. Laboratory for Information and Decision Systems, Report No. LIDS-TH-1069, 1981.

Traub, United Kingdom, Technical Literature, 1983.

Upton, D.M., and Barash, M.M., "A Grammatical Approach to Routing Flexibility in Large Manufacturing Systems," *Journal of Manufacturing Systems,* 7, pp. 209-221, 1988.

Vinod, B., and Solberg, J.J., "Optimal Machine of Flexible Manufacturing Systems," *International Journal of Production Research,* 23, pp. 1141-1151, 1985.

Warnecke, H.J., and Steinhilper, R., "Flexible Manufacturing Systems, Edp Supported Planning; Application Examples," *Proceedings of the 1 st. International Conference on Flexible Manufacturing Systems,* pp. 345-356, 1982.

Weiss, H.J., "A Greedy Heuristic for Single Machine Sequencing with Precedence Constraints, " *Management Science,* 27, # 10, pp. 1209-1216, 1981.

Whitney, C.K., and Goul, T.S., "Sequential Decision Procedures for Batching and Balancing in FMS's," *Annals of Operations Research,* 3, pp. 301-316, 1985.

Wittrock, R.J., "An Adaptable Scheduling Algorithm for Flexible Flow Lines," *Operations Research,* 36, # 3, pp. 445-453, 1988.

Yao, D.D., "Queuing Models of Flexible Manufacturing Systems," Ph.D. Dissertation, Dept. of Industrial Engineering, University of Toronto, Toronto, Ontario, 1983.

Yao, D.D., "Material and Information Flow in Flexible Manufacturing Systems," *Material Flows*(special issue in Flexible Manufacturing Systems), 1986.

Yao, D.D., and Buzacott, J.A., "Modeling the Performance of Flexible Manufacturing Systems," *International Journal of Production Research,* 23, pp. 945-960, 1985.

Yao, D.D., and Buzacott, J.A., "Modeling a Class of State Dependent Routing in Flexible Manufacturing Systems," *Annals of Operations Research,* 3, pp. 153-167, 1985.

Yao, D.D., and Kim, S.C., "Some Order relations in Closed Networks of Queues with Multiserver Stations," Technical Report, Dept. of Industrial Engineering, Columbia University, New York, 1984.

Zelenovic, D.M., "Flexibility - A Condition for Effective Production Systems," *International Journal of Production Research,* 20 no. 3, pp. 319-337, 1982.

Index

For Product Safety Concerns and Information please contact our EU
representative GPSR@taylorandfrancis.com Taylor & Francis Verlag GmbH,
Kaufingerstraße 24, 80331 München, Germany

Printed and bound by CPI Group (UK) Ltd, Croydon, CR0 4YY
08/05/2025
01864408-0003